Storytelling in
Alcoholics Anonymous

A Rhetorical Analysis

George H. Jensen

Southern Illinois University Press
Carbondale and Edwardsville

Library of Congress Cataloging-in-Publication Data
Jensen, George H.
   Storytelling in Alcoholics Anonymous : a rhetorical analysis / George H.
Jensen.
      p. cm.
   Includes bibliographical references and index.
      1. Alcoholics Anonymous. 2. Alcoholics—Rehabilitation.
   3. Communication in rehabilitation. 4. Storytelling. 5. Self-disclosure.
   I. Title.

   HV5278.J45 2000
   362.295'86—dc21
   ISBN 0-8093-2330-3 (alk. paper)   99-059912

Contents

Preface

L ong after I was an adult, my mother told me that my father had gone to Alcoholics Anonymous for six months. One day, he came home from a meeting and said, "I don't think I'm an alcoholic." I suspect that it was less than a year later—I was six—when my mother reached her breaking point and asked my father to leave. He eventually drifted to New Orleans, where he slowly drank himself to death. I have little doubt that my family was better off once my father left, even though my mother struggled to support us on a teacher's salary, but we were still an alcoholic family. I certainly thought of my own family when I read the following anecdote from *Alcoholics Anonymous:*

> The alcoholic is like a tornado roaring his way through the lives of others. Hearts are broken. Sweet relationships are dead. Affections have been uprooted. Selfish and inconsiderate habits have kept the home in turmoil. We feel a man is unthinking when he says that sobriety is enough. He is like the farmer who came up out of his cyclone cellar to find his home ruined. To his wife, he remarked, "Don't see anything the matter here, Ma. Ain't it grand the wind stopped blowin'?" (82)

The wind had stopped blowin' once my father left, but we had not experienced what members of AA or Al-Anon call recovery.

Alcoholics Anonymous describes alcoholism as a family disease, and it is ultimately the families—not just the alcoholic—who recover from an "abnormal" or "neurotic" life (122). And those families who experience recovery in AA and Al-Anon seem to move from being highly dysfunctional to being exceptionally close and well adjusted. For many years, I had respected AA as I watched close friends or relatives find sobriety by working the program, but I have been even more fascinated by the broader goals of AA. Members of AA often speak of the "dry drunk," the person who has stopped drinking but continues to be a tornado in the lives of others. Members also frequently say, "There is nothing sadder than an alcoholic who doesn't drink and is not in AA."

I thus began this project because I was intrigued by the difference between alcoholic families that were in recovery and those that were not.

When the drinker attended AA and the spouse attended Al-Anon, something dramatic happened, something that could not be accounted for simply by the absence of alcohol. The purpose of this study is to explain how such dramatic changes occur. In other words, how is it that being a member of Alcoholics Anonymous and telling one's story can contribute to the formation of a new identity?

It is this transformative effect of storytelling within Alcoholics Anonymous that is the theme of this book. As I began this project, I wanted to understand how telling life stories in AA was different from writing personal essays or autobiographies for print. I began by attending open AA and Al-Anon meetings for about three years, an average of about two a week. I wanted my rhetorical analysis to be founded on an ethnographic study of the "culture" of AA. Early in this process, I was struck by how extensively AA has entered the consciousness of popular culture (virtually everyone has heard of AA and the Twelve Steps) while relatively few people have any knowledge of what actually goes on in a meeting (they only know that someone stands up, says "Hello, I'm Bill. I'm an alcoholic," and then talks about drinking). Many people even repeat AA slogans, phrases from the Twelve Steps, or passages from AA literature, without any apparent contact with AA meetings, yet they think it's sad that members of AA have to go to so many meetings. I remember my own shock, as the son of an alcoholic, when I first heard someone say, "I am a grateful alcoholic."

The most important message of this study is that the culture of AA and its storytelling are both crucial to the transformation of identity that occurs within the program. The introduction, "Bill W.'s Story," analyzes the print version of the story told by Bill Wilson, cofounder of AA, in the first chapter of *Alcoholics Anonymous*. By employing an ethnography of reading, I will demonstrate that while Bill W.'s story serves as the paradigm for storytelling in AA, it does not adequately represent storytelling as it occurs at meetings. In other words, we cannot understand AA and its tradition of storytelling by reading and analyzing printed texts. In order to move the reader of this book (most of whom will be outsiders, not members of AA) closer to the position of an insider (someone who understands the culture and rituals of the program), I will move inductively through the next section of the book to build a sense of history and culture.

In the first section of the book, "History and Culture," I will begin with a discussion of two organizations that preceded AA: the Washingtonians and the Oxford Group. The Washingtonians, or the Washington Temperance Society, was a temperance movement that began in 1840 and was virtually defunct by 1858; the society was considered a historical lesson for AA. Bill W. believed that the Washingtonians, by becoming involved with political issues, had failed to remain focused, but other lessons can also be learned from this group. Unlike AA, they told their stories to a general public, most of whom were teetotalers. In this chapter on the Washingtonians, I will explain how appealing to a broad audience altered the organization's storytelling. In the next chapter, I will explain how AA developed within and eventually split from the Oxford Group, an interdenominational religious group that wanted to recapture the enthusiasm of first-century Christianity. Storytelling was also an important part of this organization, but its goals were to save the world and create saints. In contrast, the storytelling of AA is more about accepting one's imperfections. As readers move through these chapters, I hope they will understand something of the history of AA (common knowledge to members) as we begin to understand how storytelling in AA is quite different than that of similar movements. They will also begin to understand the storytelling of AA through counterexamples.

In the remainder of the first section, I will lead the reader through a number of chapters that will explain the culture of AA. This section, which will draw most heavily upon my experience of attending AA and Al-Anon meetings, differs stylistically from the rest of the book. Its goal is to explain important aspects of the culture of AA, to move the reader closer to the position of an insider. It is my hope that the reader, as he or she learns how meetings are structured, how printed literature is ritualized, how the Twelve Steps are worked, and how the Twelve Traditions provide unity, will undergo an initiation similar to that experienced by new members of AA during their first few weeks in the program. Of course, reading about meetings is not the same as attending them, but the reader will learn about the program and start to appreciate how its culture and rituals frame and support a unique approach to storytelling.

In "Storytelling," the second section of the book, I will use Bakhtin's theory to offer a rhetorical analysis of storytelling as it occurs within the culture of AA. By rhetorical analysis, I broadly mean any interpretation that accounts for the transactions of author, audience, and text. Bakhtinian theory is inherently rhetorical (see Bernard-Donals; Klancher; McClelland; and Schuster). Bakhtin writes of the author, the relation of the author to the text, the author's presence within the text, the hero that the author creates, the relation of the social and cultural context to both author and text, the text as an utterance in a string of utterances, the reader's interpretation of the text, and the reader's affect on the author.

In addition to his perspective on rhetorical transactions, I thought of using Bakhtin because he has written so extensively about monologic and dialogic discourse. In short, monological discourse is "single voiced" in that a particular speaker attempts to silence other speakers; it is what we most frequently encounter in our daily lives. Dialogic discourse allows multiple voices (and multiple views) to play off of each other; this was, I was finding, more typical of the talk at AA meetings. As I continued my analysis, I became more interested in two issues that are crucial to Bakhtin's theory and that became crucial to this study: How is culture related to text, and how is the author (or speaker) related to the hero (or the central character of the story)? In dealing with each issue, Bakhtin does not assume a simple correspondence. When looking at the interaction between culture and text, Bakhtin does not assume that the text is a simple reflection of its author's social setting. He looks, rather, to what might be described as a mediating concept, which he calls a chronotope. A chronotope is a way of thinking about time and space that reflects certain cultural values as well as certain literary traditions. Through this concept, Bakhtin is able to connect culture and text and avoid simplistic views, for example, that the text is merely a reflection of its social setting. When looking at the interaction between author and hero, Bakhtin wanted to avoid the equally simplistic notion, common in the biographical criticism of his day, that the author is the hero of his or her text. Bakhtin argues, in brief, that an author (whose life is still unfolding and whose character is still forming) creates a hero (whose life is finished and so can be summed up and judged). A hero, then, represents a still point in time (a value, actually) that the author answers to with his or her actions, in effect, saying, "I am becoming this hero, or I am growing away from this hero." In other words, Bakhtin's theory of the author and hero can help us to analyze and understand how speakers can create characters in their stories (make heroes of themselves as they were when they drank or as they have become since they joined AA) that can, in turn, affect the emerging identity of the speaker. In both Bakhtin's theory and the culture of AA, these are not discrete issues. A speaker (or author) cannot learn to create the kind of characters (or heroes) that bring about sobriety without understanding the chronotopes of AA narratives, which one can only learn by attending meetings. I know of no other theorist who allows for this kind of analysis.

In the second section of the book, as I analyze specific "talks" or "stories" of individual members as spoken at AA meetings, I will identify the speakers by first name and last initial, as is the tradition of anonymity within the program. I quote only from talks that have been taped and "published"—at least within AA circles through the sale of these tapes— and with the permission of the speaker. In my analysis I avoided any kind of comment that might mark individuals. After attending meetings, I took notes only about recurrent patterns, but I never took notes during meetings or in any way recorded the actual words or content of speakers. If a comment or rhetorical act did not occur repeatedly, or if a statement could potentially identify an individual, I considered it private and outside the scope and purpose of this study.

In the conclusion, I will summarize the typical talk given by a newcomer and the typical talk given by an old-timer. This discussion should clarify a central theme of the book: Members of AA change as they grow into a new way of telling their stories.

I certainly could not have completed this study without the help of a number of members of AA, Narcotics Anonymous, and Al-Anon: Ted H., Franklin W., Joe G., Mike K., Rita H., and Doug E. Special thanks to Ted H., who pointed me in a number of productive directions, loaned me books, and helped me to track down some addresses. I would also like to express my special appreciation to those members of AA who graciously allowed me to quote from tapes of their talks: Ray O'K., Gail K., Ted H., Ken D., Carolyn N., Dick M., Paul O., and Lisa B.

For reading various drafts of the manuscript, I wish to thank Etta Madden, James S. Baumlin, Ted H., Rita H., Joe G., and Mike K. Thanks to Patrick O'Reilly for help with the computer files.

For their assistance at the AA Archives in New York, I wish to thank Frank Mauser, Judit Santon, and the archive staff.

Thanks to the Stepping Stones Foundation for permission to quote from Bill W.'s unpublished letters. Special thanks to Eileen Giuliani.

For their support and love, special thanks to Donna, Jay, and Jeffrey.

Introduction

Bill W.'s Story: An Ethnography of Reading

> Our stories disclose in a general way what we used to be like, what happened, and what we are like now.
> —*Alcoholics Anonymous*

> To raise the question of the nature of narrative is to invite reflection on the very nature of culture and, possibly, even on the nature of humanity itself.
> —Hayden White, "The Value of Narrativity"

> The text as such never appears as a dead thing; beginning with any text—and sometimes passing through a lengthy series of mediating links—we always arrive, in the final analysis, at the human voice, which is to say we come up against the human being.
> —M. M. Bakhtin, "Forms of Time and Chronotope in the Novel"

The first chapter of *Alcoholics Anonymous,* affectionately known to insiders as the Big Book, is the text of Bill W.'s story. It is meant as an example, perhaps even a paradigm, for the telling of one's story in a program that began when the cofounders of AA told their stories to each other—when Bill W. told his story to Dr. Bob and Dr. Bob told his story to Bill W. But in important ways the print version of Bill W.'s story fails to capture AA storytelling within its oral tradition.[1] In the Alcoholics Anonymous program, stories are told at meetings; they are ritualized, performed, created, as one embodied voice stands before others. The book *Alcoholics Anonymous* is an important part of the culture of AA—it is, indeed, the central "sacred text"—but it hardly envelopes that culture. The culture includes the "mutually dependent and coexistent" voices that are both "in" and "around" this text (Boyarin, "Voices Around the Text" 212). In the program, stories are spoken more frequently than written and heard more frequently than read. Even when they are read, they are read within an oral tradition. And so, even as Bill W.'s story in print, given pride of place, serves to emphasize the importance of telling stories, it fails to capture the rhetoric that transforms identity.

In this chapter, in addition to foreshadowing the themes of the book, I will discuss how the storytelling in AA is part of an oral tradition that cannot be fully captured in print, but I will also argue, as part of an ethnography of reading, that the stories in print are read differently by members of the program than they are by outsiders (see Boyarin's "Jewish Ethnography" and *The Ethnography of Reading*). Writing in support of this approach to the study of reading, Fabian refers to the tendency of anthropologists to focus on texts rather than reading as "textual fundamentalism" that "obscures the nature of authorship . . . as well as the nature of reception," or reading ("Keep Listening" 89). What we will see is that outsiders, those not familiar with AA, read Bill W.'s story as an example of print autobiography and that insiders, members of AA, read Bill W.'s story through the interpretive lens of their own experiences, both their feelings about their own recoveries and their knowledge of the customs and rituals of AA meetings. Indeed, they read rituals into the text.

They might read, for example, the salutation that they have heard at meetings into the print version of Bill W.'s story. If Bill were telling his story at a meeting today, he would have been introduced and greeted by applause. Then he would have begun by saying, "Hello, I'm Bill. I'm an alcoholic."[2] The audience would have responded, "Hello, Bill." The seemingly simple exchange, an active participation between speaker and audience, would have looked odd on the page. Outsiders, as they read, would not know how to react. An exchange between speaker and audience might seem quirky, like the secret greeting of some fraternal order. Indeed, the exchange is often satirized in mass media. Within the culture of a meeting, however, this opening establishes a dialogue between speaker and audience that is repeated again and again as roles shift, as one of the audience becomes speaker and speaker becomes one of the audience—as each person, in turn, identifies himself or herself as an alcoholic. It is a seemingly simply confession that can bring a sense of relief, end isolation, or cause a speaker's gut to tighten. How can this experience be suggested in print? For insiders, it is unnecessary. They read the exchange into the text, ritualizing the story, bringing it to life, imaging themselves at a meeting with Bill W. before them, hearing their friends in the room. They may even have listened to a tape of Bill speaking, and so they might hear the timbre of his voice or the rhythm of his speech. They certainly have read portions of Bill's text aloud at group meetings. They learn to recite segments from memory before others, and so the text becomes part of their special community and part of their bodies. Svenbro has written that we often neglect the oral and bodily aspects of reading: "Reading aloud is part of the text, it is inscribed in the text. . . . [T]he text is more than the sum of the alphabetic signs of which it is made up: these signs are to guide the voice through which the text will take on a body—an audible body" (54). An oral tradition like AA is also, as Walter Ong says, more empathic and participatory: "For an oral culture learning and knowing means achieving a close empathic, communal identification with the known, 'getting with it'. Writing separates the knower from the known and thus sets up conditions for 'objectivity', in the sense of personal disengagement or distancing" (45–46).

Bill W. begins his story, as told on the pages of the Big Book, thus: "War fever ran high in the New England town to which we new, young officers from Plattsburg were assigned, and we were flattered when the first citizens took us to their homes, making us feel heroic" (1). The war metaphor will be repeated throughout his drunkolog (the drinking Bill is at war with others and at war with himself), but we also have here, in the first sentence, the central theme of AA stories: the search for a social role that one can grow into. Later in the book, I will use Bakhtin's analysis of how the author is related to the central character (referred to by Bakhtin as the hero) of a text to analyze this theme in more depth. In short, Bakhtin argues that the author (Bill) creates a character (here, the war hero) to whom he must answer (either affirm or negate) by how he lives. Bill was feeling like a hero, but he is not a war hero. He has not yet been to war. Throughout Bill's drunkolog, as is typical for this section of AA talks, Bill feels progressively more at odds with the image that he presents to the world, his persona. He changes as he begins to speak of a version of his self (a hero) that he identifies with and eventually becomes.

The dissonance between identity and role in Bill's story continues after he returns home from the war. At twenty-two, still a novice drinker, Bill began to build a career, mixing alcohol with the "inviting maelstrom of Wall Street":

> I took a night law course, and obtained employment as investigator for a surety company. The drive for success was on. I'd prove to the world I was important. My work took me about Wall Street and little by little I became interested in the market. Many people lost money—but some became very rich. Why not I? I studied economics and business as well as law. Potential alcoholic that I was, I nearly failed my law course. At one of the finals I was too drunk to think or write. Though my drinking was not yet continuous, it disturbed my wife. We had long talks when I would still her forebodings by telling her that men of genius conceived their best projects when drunk; that the most majestic constructions of philosophical thought were so derived. (*Alcoholics Anonymous* 2)

Here, Bill is not just a man feeling heroic. He is deluded, a man who expected to become important, a millionaire, while drinking heavily. The outsiders who read this story when it first appeared in 1939 might have been reminded of temperance literature. They might have seen only one path for a rummy like Bill: a slow eroding deterioration that ends in financial ruin, jail, or death. Temperance tracts, which will be discussed in a chapter on the Washingtonians, were written by "teetotalers" for other "teetotalers," who read to judge rather than empathize, to feel pride rather than identify. Maybe this is how outsiders still read Bill W.'s story. It is not how insiders read it. They and Bill W. share the same "lifeworld." Ong argues that oral cultures "conceptualize and verbalize all their knowledge with more or less close reference to the human lifeworld, assimilating the alien, objective world to the more immediate, familiar interaction of human beings" (42). Within the secondary orality of AA, there is certainly much shared knowledge between speaker and audience, and so the speaker will make comments that outsiders fail to understand. Insiders understand. They nod now and then, maybe even feel the text in the pits of their stomachs. They might imagine that they were one of the alcoholics who knew Bill, had listened to him talk about his depression or his hope at step meetings or topic meetings, who felt they knew everything about this man and that now they were hearing something new, that now they were knowing him a little better. For them, reading Bill's story is an act of participation. It is this reading or listening with a sense of identification that draws the drinker into the program. Even in the early days, Bill W. and Dr. Bob realized that the drunkolog could function as a hook for potential new members, because in this section of the story the speakers talk of how they *used to be* but also about how the newcomer *is* (Kurtz 72).

Insiders, those who are accustomed to hearing AA stories told before an audience, might also fail to notice what most outsiders would consider to be the rather flat tone of the print version of Bill's story. Insiders are accustomed to hearing those who are fairly early in their recoveries speak their drunkologs with tears or those further in recovery speak it with humor and irony. Ray O'K., an old-timer, speaking before a convention in St. Charles, Illinois, begins his story in this way:

> Let me tell you about my drinking. You don't want to miss this. It's a thrill a minute. I grew up in one of the neighborhoods in New York City and my neighborhood was rough and it was tough and it was Irish. You may not understand that here, but they drank in that neighborhood. And, if you looked at where I lived, you'd see a little drinking. My mother, the widow O'K., was known to take a drink from time to time. And when the pressure was on, Kitty would go for the light spirits, and something would fly—usually one of the children.

> My brother Billy, on the other hand, was a very bad drinker. And, in an Irish neighborhood, Billy O'K. stood out. So when I showed up at the local saloon and ordered up whatever it was they were serving fourteen year olds that afternoon, no one paid any attention to me. It was just another O'K. coming through the system. I do not recall what they served me. I suspect it was a beer. That was the neighborhood drink. But whatever it was, I liked everything about it. I liked the way it looked. I liked the way it smelled. I liked the way it tasted. I liked what it did for my head. I liked the noise and the smoke and the confusion. I liked the Irish music and the fist fights. I liked the bullshit. I really did. And I spent the next twenty years going after it. I was going through the parochial school system, in a manner of speaking. I got into all of the difficulties that you would expect a young man to get into trying to go through that system drunk. I was thrown out of high school a number of times. I held the neighborhood record for being thrown out of high school, a record previously held by my brother, Billy. (AA Talk)

Ray O'K. is having fun here, and his audience laughs at almost every phrase. As we will see, this kind of humor is both common and crucial to the AA culture, and I will return to it in a later chapter, analyzing it through Bakhtin's concept of carnival. But outsiders do not expect humor at AA meetings or in AA stories. At the 1998 Conference on College Composition and Communication, I presented the bulk of this chapter. I expected the audience to see the humor. As I had my head down reading Ray O'K.'s story, I heard no laughter. When I looked up, I saw that most of the audience had rather pained expressions on their faces. The audience, predominantly outsiders, expected tears and remorse, a serious tale with a moral.

When telling his story in print, realizing that the Big Book would be read by outsiders, Bill tells its straight—no humor or irony—even though he was known for his dark sense of humor.[3] This is not how Bill told his story before an audience, especially later in his recovery. In the following anecdote from a talk in 1960, years after the publication of the Big Book, note the humor as well as the oral qualities, the additive structure (the "and then" quality), and the sense of spontaneity. What is more difficult to convey in this transcript is Bill's inflection, which lets the audience know that he can see humor in a situation that was once an embarrassment, and his pauses, which allow the audience to respond with laughter:

> I was up in a town near my brother-in-law's place. I was supposed to show up for supper. I got talking with the man at the garage. I forgot about supper. I forgot about Lois. It was kind of a bitter night. We needed more grog to get warm. And we kept warming ourselves. Finally, I realized that I had to start for my brother-in-law's, several hours later. I started up the street and suddenly I realized it was time

> to go to bed. And, uh, there was a field and a side hill paralleling
> the street. And, uh, I wandered over in it and I laid down and it was
> a wintry night and I woke up. Gracious, I was cold. I got off it, up
> the hill to the main street, started down the street, looked down,
> and, my God, I had on my coat and my vest but no pants. Right
> down the main street of Yonkers, New York. My brother-in-law and
> Lois met me at the door. They were saddened. And since I was mi-
> nus my pants, the unspoken question was, "Where have you been?"
> (AA Talk)

When he wrote his story for the Big Book, Bill was appropriately concerned with how outsiders would react to his black humor about the worst
phase of his life. The Big Book was certainly written for members of AA,
but it was also written for outsiders—physicians, therapists, and ministers who might promote the program, and the wealthy who might do-
nate money to seed its initial growth. To these outsiders, black humor
might seem undignified. So might other emotions.

Print could hardly convey the abrupt shifts of emotion through which
an AA speaker leads an audience when they share the same room. Toward the end of Ray O'K.'s drunkolog, as he tells of his early months in
AA, he abruptly shifts from cracking jokes to a laughing audience to
sharing the worst moments of his life to a hushed crowd:

> I would drink and come to these meetings. I would come to these
> meetings and then I would drink. When I would be drinking, I cer-
> tainly never knew where I would end up once I began. It was cer-
> tainly a terrible life. And things began to happen to me that had never
> happened to me before. And I do not speak to you now of things that
> I no longer consider to be relevant or even important. I do not speak
> to you of the fact that I was dismissed from the faculty of law as a
> tenured professor of law and that all of the honors, all of the rituals,
> all of the appointments, all of the dollars that went with that posi-
> tion were taken from me in about fifteen minutes. I do not speak to
> you of the fact that I was in serious, and I mean serious, personal,
> professional and financial difficulties. I do not even mention to you
> the fact that I had lost the affection of practically everybody who
> loved me. And I spent most of my time living in a car. I do not speak
> to you of any of these things. What I say to you now is that there was,
> in my case, and perhaps in yours, a terrible, terrible disintegration of
> my spirit. That spirit that makes me different than each of you. That
> spirit that brings to this particular form whatever individuality or
> personality or character that it might have. And this was the spirit
> that once burned in me bright. And it was extinguished. (AA Talk)

In a matter of seconds, Ray O'K. moves from black humor to a tone that
might best be described as sermonic. And the audience responds with
reverence.

Throughout the rapid shifts in tone and affect in stories told at meetings, which outsiders might hear as a random string of anecdotes, there is some continuity as the speaker traces the life arc of all alcoholics.[4] The lives of alcoholics continue to fall apart as their personæ become more exaggerated. As Bill W.'s story continues, he writes of how he began to rely on alcohol more and more to bolster an increasingly inflated and unrealistic persona, a persona engaged in the rhetoric of war, killing off those around him with words. After the crash of October 1929, alcohol allows him to return to Wall Street feeling "like Napoleon returning from Elba."[5] The phrase suggests, in addition to the playing out of an archetype, that Bill W. had become lost in his social role. There is no sense here of a retreat into the ego, a reflection upon or a negation of the inflated persona. In submitting to the exaggerated importance of the individual in his culture, the need for the individual to be superior to those he competes against, Bill W. has become a social stereotype. The audience, his real audience, fellow alcoholics, know what is coming.

As his disease progresses, Bill writes of how he can no longer maintain his delusion, his wholesale acceptance of his social role, his escape from the doubts and shame of his ego. This is a key stage in many narratives about drinking, those told in AA and those told outside it. The drinking life is seen as a performance that can no longer be played convincingly.[6] The drinker becomes detached, watching himself or herself drink as if he or she were watching some other person.

At this point, Bill W. realizes that he has lost himself, that his life is falling apart, and he attempts to stop drinking. His war with others has turned inward as he begins to war with himself. The failures he faces the morning after force him to reflect on his sense of self:

> The remorse, horror and hopelessness of the next morning are unforgettable. The courage to do battle was not there. My brain raced uncontrollably and there was a terrible sense of impending calamity. I hardly dared cross the street, lest I collapse and be run down by an early morning truck, for it was scarcely daylight. An all night place supplied me with a dozen glasses of ale. My writhing nerves were stilled at last. A morning paper told me the market had gone to hell again. Well, so had I. The market would recover, but I wouldn't. That was a hard thought. Should I kill myself? No—not now. Then a mental fog settled down. Gin would fix that. So two bottles, and—oblivion.
>
> The mind and body are marvelous mechanisms, for mine endured this agony two more years. Sometimes I stole from my wife's slender purse when the morning terror and madness were on me. Again I swayed dizzily before an open window, or the medicine cabinet where there was poison, cursing myself for a weakling. (*Alcoholics Anonymous* 6)

Bill W. has found his low point. His story is still not all that different from temperance texts. Outsiders might expect his downward spiral to continue, but insiders see hope. The process of transformation, the "what happened" of his story, begins with a series of failed attempts to stop drinking. At one point, Bill thinks that "self-knowledge," his understanding with the help of a physician that alcoholism is a disease, would help him to stop drinking, but it does not. Imagine how newcomers would feel as they read this story, knowing that Bill W., the cofounder of AA, also struggled to maintain his sobriety.[7] In AA narratives, in contrast to temperance texts, sobriety does not come quickly or easily. The members of AA know this, because they interpret this text not through other texts so much but through their life experiences.

Bill W. begins his process of transformation when a friend, who had once drank as much as he but was now sober, visited. Bill W.'s friend had "got religion" and encouraged Bill to do the same.[8] Many newcomers have difficulty with this section of the narration. Most of them have either never been religious or have lost faith. Here, as he did throughout the drunkolog, Bill provides the newcomer with a character (in Bakhtin's term, a hero) to identify with, for Bill also had difficulty accepting his friend's talk of God:

> Despite the living example of my friend there remained in me the vestiges of my old prejudice. The word God still aroused a certain antipathy. When the thought was expressed that there might be a God personal to me this feeling was intensified. I didn't like the idea. I could go for such conceptions as Creative Intelligence, Universal Mind or Spirit of Nature but I resisted the thought of a Czar of the Heavens, however loving His sway might be. (12)

His friend, however, suggests that he could "choose his own conception of God," and that suggestion breaks Bill's resistance. The experience "meant destruction of self-centeredness," a destruction of the "before persona," the way he used to be.

This account of a simple meeting between Bill and his friend is the basis of the program: "one drunk telling his story to another drunk." In this pivotal moment of sharing stories, the practicing drunk stands before a recovering alcoholic and looks at the self more realistically. The persona of the practicing drunk cracks, forcing reflection. Ray O'K. describes his first encounter with AA, when in a mental institution, in this way:

> Somebody said, "You have a visitor." I didn't know who that would be, so I went into my large, executive-type padded cell and through the door came this very imposing looking man, and he said, "I'm from the Dairy Ann group of Alcoholics Anonymous," that the hospital had given up on me, and that he would like to talk to me about

> this wonderful program. I immediately reverted to my origins in the Bronx because I was up and out of my seat and I said, "Alcoholics Anonymous, what the hell, are you crazy . . ." And I started with him. And *he* told *me* to shut up. Really. I intuitively knew that they had forgotten to tell him who I was. So I decided to tell him who I was. He told me to sit down and shut up and to listen to him. Well, he was a very imposing person, and I was not a well person, and I sat, and he spun out this story. It was fascinating. (AA Talk)

It was Ray at his low point, in a mental hospital, confronted by an "imposing" and sober alcoholic who deflates his persona and begins a process of transformation. He begins to associate with recovering alcoholics and "work the steps." This is the "what happened" portion of the story, which, as O'Reilly has said, is where the "Steps are narrativized" (111), where the speaker explains the "how" of his or her transformation or simply says that the "how" cannot be explained. O'Reilly says:

> The modifying event, the "what happened" stage in AA narratives, may be related in tones that range from an awestruck gravity appropriate to the extravagance of a supernatural visitation, perhaps accompanied by upwelling tears of gratitude, to a drier kind of analytic bemusement or a detached irony. (*Sobering Tales* 120)

Bill's conversion came like a "thunderbolt"; he saw a white light. When the tales describe this kind of rapid religious conversion, outsiders might be skeptical, insiders, too. Members of AA frequently talk at meetings about how their spiritual awakenings were not like Bill's; they did not see a "burning bush." Even as they affirm that Bill's story *is* their own, they assert difference. Boyarin believes

> that far from being mutually exclusive, participation and critical awareness can and sometimes must be linked in the search for identity. This is so for any individual to the extent that she or he is dissatisfied with the founding of "modernist and post-modernist consciousness . . . on separation, on self-difference." "Alienation" cannot be overcome by denying our deeply ingrained heritage of doubt. ("Voices Around the Text" 215)

Bill W.'s story enables other alcoholics to interpret their own experiences and so opens "avenues toward understanding," but it also exerts "constraining demands" (Fabian, "Text as Terror" 173). Even though Bill W.'s dramatic spiritual awakening proved to be the exception rather than the rule, AA members struggle against the power of Bill's experience as exemplar (173). As a group, they must collectively and repeatedly state this difference. As I will discuss later, Bill himself began to downplay the significance of his conversion experience shortly after the Big Book was published. He realized by the second printing of the Big Book that his "white light" experience might exclude potential members. An appendix entitled "Spiritual Experience" was added to address this issue (569–70). He probably wrote parts of his story without realizing how *his* experience would become *the* experience.

Newcomers—even some old-timers—can also feel at odds with the "now" section of Bill's talk as they compare how they feel at the moment to Bill's general description of his life in AA. He writes about his new life, the "what we are like now" part of his story. It is almost as if Bill is now a new person in a new world, and so it is a new kind of world view (I will later tie the shift in worldview to Bakhtin's concept of chronotope) and a different narrative to go with it. He talks of "fast friends," serenity, and a new found confidence in coping with the hardships of life. Interestingly, for most of this section, he switches to "we" (and it will be "we" for the rest of the book), generalizing his experience of transformation, his "after persona," to all of the members of Alcoholics Anonymous as well as emphasizing the importance of fellowship and interpersonal relationships (we could even call it a counterculture) in maintaining the new identity. Bill may have been writing more for outsiders here, trying to sell the program, making life in the program seem better than it actually is. Newcomers often read the "now" section and think that they are far from living in some utopia; they might even doubt that they can ever grow into the kind of wonderful life that Bill describes. Old-timers who have recently relapsed or are currently struggling with their sobriety might read this section and ask, "What is wrong with me?" It might help them if they hear that Bill could not always live in the "we" of the program, in the utopia. They might be comforted if they read Fitzgerald's *The Soul of Sponsorship* and learn that Bill W. himself was often depressed, even after years of sobriety (33). They begin to understand that the Bill W. described in the "now" sections is a persona (a hero) that Bill himself strove to become.

Bill W.'s story in print is both like and unlike the stories that one hears at meetings. It reads like autobiography. It is a crafted narrative that has a beginning, middle, and end; it is arranged in chronological order. The stories spoken at meetings rarely achieve this kind of coherence. An excerpt from Gail K.'s story illustrates how events need not be ordered chronologically or thematically. The excerpt comes from the middle of about a thirty minute talk. It includes elements of how she "used to be," "what happened," and how she "is now," but not in strict chronological order and not in a polished prose:

> I was so miserable that I had to do something. I had to change something. And I didn't know what it was that needed to be changed. I really didn't even put together, until I was in a treatment center, that

alcohol was part of my problem. And then I found out that alcohol was my true solution to my problem, which was me. And now today I know that, when I'm upset, there's something wrong with me. You know. And I don't like that, but it's the truth. God has given me blessings in this program with my children. All I can say is that, behaviorwise, there is no comparison to what it used to be like. I used to try to be a mother, but I didn't know how. I didn't know how to be strong when I needed to be. And I was too soft when I didn't need to be. I didn't know how to live, so I didn't know how to be a mom, I didn't know how to be a wife. I didn't know much of anything but how to drink, how to run around, and how to be nuts. And I had plenty of opportunity to do that. I've been in and out of mental institutions, in and out of treatment centers, twice. Thank God, the second time . . . I say it was enough, but it wasn't enough, the second treatment, but something happened to me. And I know it was God. After the second treatment, something happened to me and I just got a new awakening of sobriety and suddenly I wanted it. I really wanted it. (AA Talk)

The stories told in AA meetings are not written and then read to a sleepy audience. They are created on the spot. They are fragmentary, incoherent, incomplete. The stories themselves might lack plot, but the audience can bring a sense of order to the story. They bring the "plot" of their life experiences and the "plot" of Bill W.'s story.

In the Big Book, one finds little advice on how to tell one's story. Speakers are supposed to "share their experience, strength and hope" and "share in a general way what we used to be like, what happened, and what we are like now" (58). The stories usually have three key components: "what we used to be like," the days of drinking, also referred to as the drunkolog; "what happened," or how the speaker came to AA and how the speaker began to transform his or her identity; and "what we are like now," how the speaker's life has changed for the better and what it is like to be a member of AA. Bill W.'s story moves through these elements in chronological order, as do the more polished talks of old-timers or circuit speakers (the more entertaining and proficient speakers who are frequently invited to speak at conventions and special events),[9] but most talks, especially those of newcomers, make scattered hits upon these themes in a rather random order. Gail K. speaks in this order of how she "was so miserable" (then), knowing she had to change something and being in treatment centers (coming to AA), how she deals with being upset today (now), blessings and changed behavior (now), not knowing how to live (then), and more about treatment centers (coming to AA). More typical of AA talks, Gail does not move in an orderly progression through how she used to be, what happened, and how she is now. Contrary to printed autobiography, she tells her story in a general way, more in the tradition of orality.[10] Comments like "I didn't know how to be a mom" pass without elaboration or corroborating detail. She is composing her story on the spot. The word "twice" is added to the following sentence as an afterthought: "I've been in and out of mental institutions, in and out of treatment centers, twice." Or notice how she shifts direction in the following sentence: "Thank God, the second time, I say it was enough, but it wasn't enough, the second treatment, but something happened to me." After the phrase "the second time," she seems to have thought but did not say "was enough," which she then qualifies, "I say it was enough, but it wasn't enough." In Gail's story, which is more typical of what one hears at an AA meeting, there is a sense that she is finding herself and her way *as* she speaks. In the early days of the Akron group, which Dr. Bob formed, members did not even know in advance whether or not they would tell their stories that night. One new member, when selected to speak, complained, "But I didn't prepare anything." Dr. Bob replied, "You didn't prepare to get drunk, either. Get up and talk" (*Dr. Bob* 223). O'Reilly writes:

> The object of hearing oneself speak is a concept that lies somewhere between the free association of psychoanalysis and automatic writing, between therapy and poetry. The double prescription of honesty and spontaneity in AA is universally endorsed, reckoned a sine qua non for "comfortable" sobriety; and the AA meeting, like the psychoanalytic session, becomes a "facilitating environment" for the nurturing of the "reflective self-awareness" that is required for generative explorations of the self. (*Sobering Tales* 137)

This is part of the magic of telling one's story—being surprised.

Bill W. must have realized, when he drafted the Big Book, that he had to show the importance of telling one's story, but he probably also struggled with how to convey that experience in print, especially to the newcomers who had not yet come to know the program's rituals or to outsiders who might be all too ready to judge. He began the Big Book with his story, moved into an analysis of how the program works, then ended with the stories of Dr. Bob and others. Despite its arrangement to emphasize the importance of telling stories, the Big Book is still a book. It can serve the function of a sacred text, unifying a culture, identifying members, playing a role in rituals, but it could not possibly embody the program. It could not fully convey what it means to speak one's story to an audience within a ritualized setting.

Part One

History and Culture

1

The Washingtonians: Telling Stories to Teetotalers

> I wish every AA could indelibly burn the history of the "Washingtonian" into his memory. It is an outstanding example of how, and how not, we ought to conduct ourselves.
> —Bill W. to Milton A. Maxwell, August 12, 1950

> The Washingtonians almost succeeded as a fellowship of alcoholics. But they had no definite program of spiritual activity and after a time got entangled in the wet-dry controversy, abolition of slavery and the like. They had mass meetings and "name" speakers. There was no anonymity. These counter forces regrettably disintegrated them. Early in A.A. we became aware of this and have, I hope, avoided their mistakes.
> —Bill W. to Spence, June 18, 1962

The Massachusetts Society for the Suppression of Intemperance, the first temperance organization in the United States, was founded in 1813 to curb excessive drinking and the use of hard spirits—its elite members, largely clergy and wealthy businessmen, enjoyed their wine—and to malign working-class drunkards. By 1826 the American Temperance Society was founded, primarily through the work of minister Justin Edwards, as the first national organization devoted to the cause. Soon, by 1833, approximately six thousand temperance organizations had been formed in the country, with a collective membership of around one million (Dannenbaum 16–20). As the organizations proliferated, more "common men" became members. They pushed for "teetotalism," in opposition to the wishes of upper-class factions, and began to associate the temperance movement with a broader social agenda, including "the eradication of all social imperfections as a prelude to the arrival of the millennium" (Dannenbaum 22). They did not consider the use of spirits to be the only evil of society, but they did believe that it was a dangerously disruptive force to community and family.[1]

Widely distributed pamphlets on the dangers of drinking, published by the American Temperance Society and other temperance groups, soon developed into a diverse range of temperance literature. The works of Timothy Shay Arthur, one of the more prolific temperance writers, accounted by some estimates for 5 percent of all fiction sold in the United States between 1840 and 1850 (Holman vii). Nadelhaft points out that temperance literature reflected—perhaps also influenced—a change in the American family away from male dominance:

> Early in the nineteenth century, the ideal of the family began to change. More and more, literature setting forth the proper standards of behavior argued for the morality of the companionate marriage. Men were no longer to rule by force or simply by the authority granted to the "superior sex." They were to be sweet partners with their wives, complementing them in the conduct of their joint responsibilities. (19)

It was temperance literature that first brought public attention to wife abuse (15), yet the literature reflected a dark side as well. In "Temperance in the Bed of a Child," Sánchez-Eppler describes how the intemperate father is typically saved by the caresses of his young daughter, a scene often depicted as occurring in the bed of the daughter. These scenes, she feels, portray thinly veiled sexual abuse as they simultaneously argue for the virtues of temperance.

This odd mixture of morality and perversity—perhaps unavoidable when authors played to a wide and diverse audience—was typical of the reform movements that permeated American culture of the time. Reynolds divides the broader coterie of reform literature into two categories: conventional and subversive. While both groups were "ostensibly based upon an interest in preserving moral and physical healthiness," the conventional texts emphasized "the ingredients and rewards of virtue rather than the wages of sin" (58). Sarah Savage's *The Factory Girl* (1814), for example, says little about the difficulties of factory work but emphasizes "the blissful home, the nurturing parent, the angelic child, the idyllic village environment, and self-improvement through hard work and moral discipline" (Reynolds 58). The subversive reform literature, on the other hand, focused on the "wages of sin." This literature is a "culture," Reynolds says, "of shifting boundaries" between reform and vice; it is difficult "to decide when certain warring parties have slipped into the enemy's territory" (59). The subversive form of temperance literature that purportedly wished to reform prostitution was accused of being pornographic, that directed toward reform of slavery was accused of having sadomasochistic undercurrents, and that directed toward reform of drink was accused of reveling in all forms of illicit behavior. In general, the subversive reform literature, which sold quite well, allowed those ordinary citizens who were attempting to lead "moral" lives to peer into the dark sides of humanity and, perhaps, their own dark sides as well. Reynolds writes:

> The paradoxical combination of the perverse and the prudish is typified by Weems's tracts *The Drunkard's Looking Glass* and *God's Revenge Against Adultery*. Both works end with sober essays calling for improved education and stricter blue laws. The illustrative tales that precede these essays, however, are so filled with violence and eroticism that we can have little doubt Weems was fascinated with the abominations he pretended to decry. (60)

It was amid this zealous reform movement and its controversies that the Washington Temperance Society, known as the Washingtonians, was formed. When six intemperate men gathered at a tavern in Baltimore on April 5, 1840, to form the group, they were certain of one thing: They did not want a society like existing temperance organizations.[2] Sermons and moral lectures, they realized, could not reform drunkards. In a book published anonymously, John Zug wrote:[3]

> The addresses made at temperance meetings, were rather of a tendency to drive away the drinking man, and those engaged in the manufacture and traffic of intoxicating liquors. And even if the ridicule or denunciation of drunkenness did not constitute the burden of the former temperance speeches, mere general lectures on moral duty however just in themselves, were not likely to reach the man, whose mind was beclouded and whose heart was seared by strong drink. It was of little avail to argue with him of the moral obligation of setting a good example—of the operation of Christian charity, in inducing a willingness to make sacrifices for our own good, and the good of others—to prove that the Bible sanctioned neither drunkenness, nor even the moderate use of alcoholic drinks—to present to him the chemical and physiological view of the question, and show him that alcohol was poison, &c., &c. He cared not for these things. (37–38)

In opposition to the religious approach to temperance, the Washingtonians formed an organization that was remarkably similar to Alcoholics Anonymous as it would independently develop in the next century. The only qualification for membership was a commitment to total abstinence, although members were expected to adhere to a basic principle: Avoid politics and religion. New members took a pledge—agreeing as gentlemen to stop drinking—and they believed in "good works," that is, becoming missionaries for the cause. Their book ends: "Save yourself, and save others. Remember that you are accountable, here and hereafter, for the man who stumbles over your example into a drunkard's grave!" (67). They even viewed excessive drinking as a disease and felt their best hope was in a fellowship of intemperate men, as reflected in their motto: "We be brethren; let us not fall out by the way" (21). And, most importantly, they would not give sermons. They would, instead, speak of their experiences, drawing upon "common sense" and "common honesty." Zug wrote: "A reformed drunkard's experience touches a chord, that vibrates in every human breast. Moreover the drunkard when reformed best knows how to reach the drunkard's heart; for he best understands his feelings" (65). Meetings were devoted to relating "personal experiences"; as members listened, "their hearts vibrated together" (12). Stories were even a part of their missionary work:

> Immediately after the organization of the society, the several members went privately to their friends, especially their former drinking associates, and persuaded them in the spirit of kindness, to abandon strong drink, and join the society. To every excuse and plea that they could not reform, they would reply by referring to their own experience. (15)

Zug's description of the early Washingtonians does not give a sense for how it functioned as members began to tell their stories to large public meetings, as their stories became more like temperance tracts. The following from the *New York Commercial Advertiser,* an account of the first Washingtonian meeting in New York on March 23, 1841, reflects the passion of the meetings and the public interest they drew:

> During the first speech a young man arose in the gallery and, though intoxicated, begged to know if there was any hope for him; declaring his readiness to bind himself, from that hour, to drink no more. He was invited to come down and sign the pledge, which he did forthwith, in the presence of the audience, under deep emotion, which seemed to be contagious, for others followed; and during each of the speeches they continued to come forward and sign, until more than a hundred pledges were obtained; a large proportion of which were intemperate persons, some of whom were old and gray headed. Such a scene as was beheld at the secretary's table while they were signing, and the unaffected tears that were flowing, and the cordial greeting of the recruits by the Baltimore delegates, was never before witnessed in New York. (qtd. in Maxwell, "Washingtonian" 417–18)

In short time, the Washingtonians attracted such attention for their mass meetings that the American Temperance Society and other temperance groups drew them into their ranks. The Washingtonians and their speakers eventually became a mass public spectacle. On May 28, 1844, they sponsored a meeting that reportedly drew thirty thousand people, most of them members of various temperance groups rather than members of the Washingtonians, and most of them teetotalers rather than reformed drunkards (Maxwell, "Washingtonian" 424). The principles that Zug presented in his book, while perhaps an accurate description of the early activities of the Baltimore chapter, may say little of the later Washingtonians, a sideshow for a broader temperance movement.

In the lore of AA, the Washingtonians involvement with politics—in particular, the slavery issue—is most often cited as the cause of the organization's demise, but Reynolds claims its association with the broader reform movement, including its darker side, may have also affected its storytelling.[4] Most prominently, the rhetoric of John Bartholomew Gough, who developed a career as a Washingtonian lecturer, Reynolds recounts, fed upon the general public's voyeuristic concern for the less fortunate:

> The most notorious of the Washingtonians was John Bartholomew Gough, the "poet of the d.t.'s." The most successful temperance lecturer of the 1840s, Gough was always surrounded by controversy; he was repeatedly charged with tawdry lecture tactics, with excessive emphasis on the grisly details of alcoholism rather than the cure for it, and, most damaging of all, with drinking and whoring on the sly himself. Gough loved to tell horror stories about crazed drunkards, such as that of a drunken man so annoyed by the crying of his two-year-old daughter that he roasted the girl over an open fire. As an alcoholic earlier in life, Gough had suffered often from delirium tremens, and his addresses were filled with reports of his nightmarish visions of terrible faces, bloated insects, oceans of blood, hundred-bladed knives tangled in his skin, and so on. A trained actor and singer, Gough raised many eyebrows with his temperance histrionics and once admitted: "I have been called 'humbug,' a 'theatrical performer,' a 'mountebank,' a 'clown,' a 'buffoon.'" Like other immoral reformers before and after him, Gough seemed drawn to the very vices he denounced. He became the focus of a national scandal in 1845, when, after disappearing for a week, he was found in a New York whorehouse, apparently grossly drunk. Gough denied any wrongdoing, claiming he had been carried unconscious to the whorehouse after he had accidently swallowed drugged cherry soda, but newspapers throughout the nation discarded his story as a transparent lie and branded him as a dissolute hypocrite. Although Gough continued to be a successful temperance lecturer for several decades, the Washingtonian cause was sullied by the scandal, and temperance as a whole became another reform movement poisoned by the paradox of immoral didacticism. (67–68)

Gough's relapse may have temporarily harmed the Washingtonians, but Reynolds, I believe, overstates the damaging effect of Gough's relapse.[5] Gough continued an exceptionally successful career as a speaker, both in the United States and abroad. His autobiography was revised several times, and his lectures continued to be printed. Maxwell argues more convincingly that the force of the Washingtonians was dissipated by its association and conflict with the temperance movement, especially the American Temperance Union, and by its splintering into groups such as the Order of the Sons of Temperance and the Cadets of Temperance ("Washingtonian" 437–43). Maxwell also argues that the later Washingtonians, as the organization developed in the temperance movement, did not have a comprehensive program for helping alcoholics, such as AA's Twelve Steps:

> Their approach to the problem of alcoholism and alcohol was moralistic rather than psychological or therapeutic. They possessed no program for personality-change. The group had no source of ideas to help them rise above the ideational content locally possessed. Except for their program of mutual aid they had no pattern of organization or activity different from existing patterns. There was far too great a reliance upon the pledge, and not enough appreciation of other elements in their program. Work with other alcoholics was not required, nor was the therapeutic value of this work explicitly recognized. (444)

I would add that the Washingtonians, as they told their stories to larger and more varied audiences, lost touch with the therapeutic value of telling one's story. Their later storytelling was to and for an audience, overtly as moral suasion and covertly as a dark entertainment, rather than to promote personal growth.

While Gough's sensational relapse may not have appreciably harmed the Washingtonians, his talks do illustrate how Washingtonian speakers were shaped by their audience. As Bakhtin says, "the role of the *others* for whom the utterance is constructed is extremely great." He adds: "From the very beginning, the speaker expects a response from them, an active responsive understanding. The entire utterance is constructed, as it were, in anticipation of encountering this response" ("Problem of Speech Genres" 94). A Washingtonian speaking before other Washingtonians is quite different than a Washingtonian speaking before teetotalers. The need to persuade or entertain seems to have encouraged the development of "name" speakers who could, like Gough, draw large crowds and titillate them with an unhealthy attention to detail. In AA, where "one drunk talks to another," stories are told "in a general way," without narrative detail (*Alcoholics Anonymous* 58). Given that Washingtonians were soon telling their stories to people who were not themselves drinkers, they had to narrate their experiences in detail, both to explain a reality that the audience had not lived through themselves and to entertain. This style of speaking evoked an intensity of passion that, no doubt, contributed to its rapid growth in membership as well as its rapid demise. That kind of passion, which could be compared to the intense and short-lived discharge of emotion during the Great Awakening (see White's *Puritan Rhetoric*), appears to run its course quickly.[6]

The same appeal to a broad audience can be seen in the published version of Washingtonian stories, written by T. S. Arthur. Arthur's *Temperance Tales* purports to be an accurate account of the "sad experiences" shared "only a few months after the formation of the original Washington Temperance Society" (iv). He claims to have attended these early meetings, presenting the tales within quotations as if he were the mere recorder and not the author. They are, however, clean narratives (the actual tales told by the Washingtonians were almost certainly more oral, i.e., more spontaneous); each tale is similar to the others in style and content, similar as well to Arthur's later *Ten Nights in a Bar-Room,* his most popular temperance novel. Both volumes present tales of victimization—the most common theme of the sentimental novel and melodrama.

"The Drunkard's Wife," which appears in the second volume of *Temperance Tales,* begins with a narrative frame, the opening of a meeting of the Washingtonians and a call to sign the pledge:

> "Think of your wives and little ones!" said the President, while making one of his stirring appeals to the crowd that filled the hall at which meetings of the Washingtonians were held. "Think of the pale, care-worn face of her you promised, many years ago, to love and to cherish! Think of the dear ones whose young innocent affections once twined about your heart, and whose glad voices once rung in your ears like the tones of sweetest music!" (2: 1)

In this frame is the message of each tale: Alcohol destroys perfect women and children. The story then moves into a third person narration of Grace Harper, whose husband, a promising doctor, develops a drinking problem.[7] He starts innocently by accepting drinks, hospitably offered by the families that he visits on his rounds; the narrator's moralizing is apparent even before drinking begins to destroy the doctor's career and family:

> Of danger he did not, of course, dream. Then strong drink was not known as the seeming friend that woos and delights until it has gained power and influence, when it unmasks itself, and proves the bitterest and most subtle enemy that man has to contend with. He looked upon it as a good, and used it as such. (2: 5)

The moral descent foreshadowed in the narration of Dr. Harper's first drink unfolds rapidly. He soon abuses his wife and children when intoxicated and feels shame when sober; the narrator and the audience, as Arthur fashions the tale, remain aloof. The wife and children are described as being without fault, perfect victims who might warrant pity from the audience. In this particular tale, the wife is constant and loyal, a voice of reason caught up in the maelstrom of another's drinking. When Dr. Harper asks his wife to attend a dinner party with him, her response is measured:

> "If you wish me to go with you, I will go, of course," was the reply. "But I cannot feel that I would be doing right to you, without using every reason in my power to induce you to stay away. Had you seen the effect of your appearance and condition on Mr. Mabury and his company, as I saw, on the evening of your last visit, you would not dream of going to-night. Every one's enjoyment was marred, and I felt as if I would gladly have shrunk into nothingness. Do not, then, expose yourself again nor throw upon your wife, who loves you, a burden so hard to bear! If all this seems strange to you, think why it is that Mr. Mabury sent for Doctor Elwell last week, to attend his little girl. There must be some good reason why he did not call you in." (2: 16)

Her remarks bring Dr. Harper "to his feet with a look of surprise, concern, and mortification on his countenance."[8]

As his drinking becomes more excessive, even Dr. Harper begins to realize the effects and attempts repeatedly to stop, but he cannot stop alone—a consistent theme of these tales. It is only when a friend takes him to a meeting of the Washingtonians, only once he has signed the pledge, that he can stop drinking. And, as with all these tales, once the pledge is signed, his sobriety is immediate and final. Relapses occur when the drinker attempts to quit on his own but never after he has joined the Washingtonians. Then, as with all of the tales, Arthur presents an idealized ending:

> And they were again happy. Doctor Harper was not mistaken in the power of association. Up to this time, he has not only kept his pledge, but is one among the most active members of the temperance society. He has resumed the practice of medicine, and is fast acquiring confidence, and we doubt not will yet rise to eminence in his profession. (2: 45)

In basic structure, these tales are similar to print versions of AA stories. They move through three basic stages: drunkolog, coming to the fellowship, and the new life in sobriety. But there are major differences. In AA, the drunkolog is typically told with humor or irony (not as tales of victimization), coming to the fellowship is a difficult process (marked by struggles and relapses), and sobriety is a time of learning to deal with the problems of life without alcohol (in contrast to both temperance tales and the print version of Bill W.'s story). Ken D., in a passage that is more typical of stories told at AA meetings, says of the early days in the program:

> And as you're here longer and you get more and more of life in a
> sober vein, you find out there's a lot of life that goes on and things
> happen to you whether you're sober or not. There's a loss of inno-
> cence. Because when you're new, you tend to think, "Gee, I'm do-
> ing all of these good things, obviously nothing can go wrong." And
> things do go wrong. That's just life. (AA Talk)

When we read Arthur's versions of the Washingtonian tales through the
lens of AA stories, they seem too ordered and idealized. They seem to
have more of Arthur's pen—and the judgment of teetotalers—than the
early voice of the Washingtonians.

Yet, the most significant difference between Arthur's version of the
Washingtonian tales and AA stories has to do with the relationship between speaker (or writer), listener (or reader), and hero (the speaker's
characterization of self within the tale). Todorov suggests that the transformation in the hero upon which narratives turn can be either *mytho-
logical* (dealing with action) or *gnoseological* (dealing with insight or
knowledge). Of *La Quête du Graal*, a narrative that begins with the audience knowing all of the significant action, he writes:

> The reader's interest is not driven by the question What happens
> next?, which refers us to the logic of succession or to the mythological
> narrative. We know perfectly well from the start what will happen,
> who will reach the Grail, who will be punished and why. Our inter-
> est arises from a wholly different question which refers instead to
> the gnoseological organization: What is the Grail? The Grail narra-
> tive relates a quest; what is being sought, however, is not an object
> but a meaning, the meaning of the word Grail. And since the ques-
> tion has to do with being and not with doing, the exploration of the
> future is less important than that of the past. Throughout the nar-
> rative the reader has to wonder about the meaning of the Grail. The
> principal narrative is a narrative of knowledge; ideally, it would never
> end. (33)

Certainly, both Arthur's tales and AA tales are gnoseological in the sense
that the drinker learns, at some point, that he (and they are all male) must
stop drinking. This is, however, the only knowledge learned in Arthur's
tales. The reader (most of whom were women) begins the narrative knowing that *drinking always leads to personal disaster;* the reader finishes the
tale and learns only that *drinking always leads to personal disaster.* In
other words, the reader only reconfirms what she already knew. So, we
might ask, as Todorov does not, what purpose do such tales serve? Perhaps as the reader reinforces existing beliefs, she *also* reinforces her status in relation to the hero of the tale: The point of these tales is that the
hero changes so that the reader can remain the same. The poor drunkard can be pitied as the reader watches his life unravel, and he can be

regarded with parental praise—lacquered with a heavy coat of condescension—when he reforms, as he transforms himself into a person who is more like the reader. The reader remains self-righteous, feeling no need to change herself.

In AA stories, as will be explained in subsequent chapters, speakers tell of insights learned during their journeys to and through recovery. The listeners, also alcoholics, commune with the speakers and are transformed by their stories. This is quite distinct from "teetotalers" reading temperance tales. Arthur's version of the Washingtonian tales certainly owes a great deal to the emerging traditions of sentimental women's fiction (writers like Catharine Maria Sedgwick, Sarah Josepha Hale, Sarah Susanna Cummins, and Susan Warner wrote, as did temperance authors, for a growing audience of women readers) and melodrama (Arthur's *Ten Nights in a Bar-Room* was adapted into a popular stage play); both of these genres portray heroes and heroines on the verge of personal disaster. In Arthur's temperance literature, even in the tales he claims to have truthfully recorded from meetings of the Washingtonians, the hero is lost in the plot. To evoke the greatest sympathy from the reader, the suffering of innocents is emphasized. Even the hero is a victim. He is a fine man until he takes his first sip, and then his life begins to fall apart.[9] Alcohol might easily be replaced by a villain, a flood, or a financial disaster. In his *Temperance Tales,* the stories of the Washingtonians end happily—as in melodramas—when the hero is saved at the last minute. No more than a paragraph or two is wasted on the perfect life that ensues with sobriety and a fellowship with the Washingtonians. In other temperance tales, it is the same. The stories are about surviving personal disaster rather than coming to knowledge of the self. In T. S. Arthur's *Ten Nights in a Bar-Room,* the narrator describes his scattered visits to a tavern, marking the deterioration of the owner and his family, the building, and everyone who enters it. One section reads:

> It is rarely, I believe, that wives consent freely to the opening of taverns by their husbands; and the determination on the part of the latter to do so, is not unfrequently attended with a breach of confidence and good feeling, never afterward fully healed. Men look close to the money result; women to the moral consequences. I doubt if there be one dram-seller in ten, between whom and his wife there exists a good understanding—to say nothing of genuine affection. And, in the exceptional cases, it will generally be found that the wife is as mercenary, or careless of the public good, as her husband. I have known some women to set up grog-shops; but they were women of bad principles and worse hearts. I remember one case, where a woman, with a sober, church-going husband, opened a dram-shop. The husband opposed, remonstrated, begged, threatened—but all to no purpose. The wife, by working for the clothing stores, had earned

and saved about three hundred dollars. The love of money, in the slow process of accumulation, had been awakened; and, in ministering to the depraved appetites of men who loved drink and neglected their families, she saw a quicker mode of acquiring the gold she coveted. And so the dram-shop was opened. And what was the result? The husband quit going to church. He had no heart for that; for, even on the Sabbath day, the fiery stream was stayed not in his house. Next he began to tipple. Soon, alas! the subtle poison so pervaded his system that morbid desire came; and then he moved along quick-footed in the way of ruin. In less than three years, I think, from the time the grog-shop was opened by his wife, he was in a drunkard's grave. A year or two more, and the pit that was digged for others by the hands of the wife, she fell into herself. Ever breathing an atmosphere, poisoned by the fumes of liquor, the love of tasting it was gradually formed, and she, too, in the end, became a slave to the Demon of Drink. She died, at last, poor as a beggar in the street. Ah! this liquor-selling is the way to ruin; and they who open the gates, as well as those who enter the downward path, alike go to destruction. But this is digressing. (28–29)

This is not really a digression. It is the tale within a tale, each telling and retelling the same story: The first drink leads to a downward spiral from which no one is saved.[10] What does the reader feel? The reader feels pity for the less fortunate, righteousness for the self.

2

The Oxford Group: The Stories of Saints

So far as I am concerned, and Dr. Smith too, the O[xford]. G[roup]. seeded AA. It was our spiritual wellspring at the beginning.

—Bill W. to Sam Shoemaker, July 14, 1949

Rowland H. played an important role in the history of AA, but we do not know much of his story. He never spoke at an AA conference. He never wrote about his contribution to AA. What we do know are some unadorned facts. Rowland was in therapy with Carl Jung (actually, it was his second trip to the master) when he asked if he could ever be cured of alcoholism. Dr. Jung was brutally honest. He told Rowland that cases like his were typically hopeless. Jung then said that he had seen some rare cases who had been cured of alcoholism through a religious conversion.

When Rowland was returning from Vienna, he found what he needed, a religious awakening of sorts, while he was reading A. J. Russell's *For Sinners Only*, a book about the Oxford Group. It was then through the storytelling in the Oxford Group and his association with Dr. Samuel Shoemaker that Rowland was able to find sobriety (Kurtz 9). He passed this message on to Ebby, who passed it on to Bill W., who passed it on to Dr. Bob.[1]

So how could Rowland, this hopeless case, experience a religious conversion while reading a book? Maybe the only way to even suggest an answer is to read *For Sinners Only* through Rowland's eyes, through the eyes of a skeptic who needed to believe in miracles, who came to believe in a religious movement that was the very antithesis of modern skepticism. In *What Is the Oxford Group?*, written by "The Layman with a Notebook," an anonymous member of the Oxford Group, the author writes:

> The aims of the Oxford Group are to bring into the world the real-
> ization of the power of the Holy Spirit as a force for spiritual and
> material stability and betterment of the world; to awaken in us as
> individuals the knowledge that we are dissipating our spiritual in-
> heritance and that Sin is the frustration of God's Plan for us all. It
> sets out to make the world understand that spiritual common sense
> is of more practical value and use to mankind than selfish piety or
> blind paganism. (6)

The Group's wish to return to "first century Christianity" was viewed, expressly by members, as a reaction to the "modern age" and the things "we moderns believe" (55), especially positivism and Freudianism, as well as an attempt to recapture a more spiritual and dedicated form of Christianity. A book about a first-century approach to Christianity would seem to be an unlikely source of inspiration for Rowland, until we realize that *For Sinners Only* is written for skeptics.

For Sinners Only is a book of stories within stories. The meta-story is Russell's own, his desire to fight through the natural skepticism of a newspaper man and find a spiritual answer. As Russell slowly tells his own story, the story of writing a series of newspaper articles on the Oxford Group and its leader, Frank Buchman, he also tells of his slow development of faith. He gives hints of miracles, suggestions that something wonderful began at Oxford University that quickly spread around the world. But we only see glimpses of the hope, for Russell is slow to believe. He doesn't want to be taken in, he doesn't want to perpetuate a fraud on the readers of his newspaper. Reading the book, and maybe this is what Rowland experienced, is like riding down the road at sixty miles an hour with a driver who keeps slamming on the brakes. A hint of miracles, then doubts, more hints, and even more doubts. Russell's doubts crash headlong into the stories of the movement changing lives, often stories about Frank bringing a lost soul to the movement. In this book about a movement that wanted to recreate the dedication of first-century Christianity, we learn about Frank as we learn about Jesus, through the stories of his followers. The skeptical reader, maybe Rowland also, finds himself or herself fighting against Russell's doubts, wanting more about miracles, more about Frank, more about the movement, without even realizing that his or her own doubts are slowly dissolving.

Russell begins to tell about Frank in chapter 4 by paraphrasing Harold Begbie's *Life-Changers,* another book of stories about the Oxford Group. Frank's own story is there, noted simply and anonymously as "F.B." This first glimpse of the miracle worker is, similar to the rest of the book, framed by levels of skepticism:

> Harold Begbie scored several successes before he wrote *Life-Chang-
> ers,* including (so everyone said) *Mirrors of Downing Street,* a col-

lection of piquant sketches of the men around King George V during the Great War, but hiding his authorship under the pen-name "A
Gentleman with a Duster." One or two celebrities received a severe
"dusting-down," possibly not altogether deserved, from the "Gentleman with a Duster." I knew a few of them. (39)

Here we have a skeptic (Russell) telling about another skeptic (Begbie)
telling about a believer. Later, when Russell first meets Frank, he shares
his plan to write an article about the movement. Frank tells Russell that
"the Holy Spirit's guidance" was opposed to Russell writing about the
movement until he was "spiritually ready for the task." Russell's reaction is typical of the early portions of the book: "For a time I wondered
if Frank's uncomplimentary attitude was not merely clever charlatanism,
an effort to hoodwink me by quoting the Holy Spirit, to ensure that we
only published what he wanted, irrespective of our honest convictions
about his teachings" (89). Rowland might have felt that if Russell could
believe, if Begbie could believe, maybe he too could believe. *For Sinners
Only* even tells a story of nonbeliever and alcoholic Bill Pickle, who came
to believe and stopped drinking.

Once Rowland began to move past his initial doubts, he was probably also fascinated by some of the basic beliefs of the Oxford Group,
beliefs that would later find their place in AA: their surrender to God,
their sharing of stories, their daily time of prayer and meditation, their
seeking of guidance, their making of amends for past wrongs.[2] This would
all sound familiar to someone who had been in therapy with Carl Jung.
Dr. Jung had his own spirit guide, whom he contacted through guided
imagery; therapy was a kind of confession, and the notion of making
amends is similar to Jung's notion of coming to terms with one's shadow.

The shadow, in Jung's system, is the dark side of one's personality. It
is the part of us that we cannot accept, that has no place in the "good"
identity of our inflated egos, so we suppress it. In its life in the unconscious, the shadow is beyond our control. It emerges, erupts, possesses
us, in those moments when we act contrary to our character. It is the devil
within us all that we cannot control. The first major step in personal
development, Jung believed, was to become conscious of one's shadow,
to realize that we are not as good as we thought.

The way that Russell speaks of public confessions and making amends
suggests something of this process, but *For Sinners Only* does read, at
times, like hagiography, a book that makes a saint of Frank Buchman as
Buchman guides others to sainthood, even a book about how the reader
as well can become a saint. Russell speaks of how Frank wants people
to become aware of their weaknesses so that they can eliminate them.
Russell recounts how Frank urged him "to drive stakes" around himself

"as protection against further lapses" (94). He continues: "Frank's drive to get me to forsake every form of sin and to put an unscalable fence between it and me caught me unawares, although I should have been ready for him after reading of his tactics" (94). According to the author of *What Is the Oxford Group?*, Buchman started the organization after he had "a vision of a Christ-led world untrammeled by Sin" (13), and so he includes an entire chapter on sin that reacts to the redefinition of sin by psychoanalysis:

> Sin and temptation to Sin are called by the modern intelligentsia any name but their own. To these "high-brows" sins are repressed desires; inhibitions; fixations; morbid introspections; suppression of natural instincts and other words ending in "ism", "phobia", "mania"—anything but what they are—just plain Sin. (20)

It is, perhaps, this focus on sin that hinders Frank Buchman—and others in the Oxford Group—from understanding the concept of a shadow. In a chapter entitled "The Stung Conscience," Russell relates a story that is a fine illustration of the shadow:

> Canon Grenstead told me the story of two temperate ladies who indulged in champagne for the first time. Presently one of them leaned over to the other and exclaimed:
> "You're drunk! You've got two noses."
> "That," said the Bampton Lecturer, "was just a clear case of projection. Drunk herself, she was accusing the other person." (260)

We often, Jung says, project our dark side onto others. Russell seems to understand this, but then he writes of how those who criticize the Oxford Group have a "stung conscience"; they are, though he does not use quite these words, projecting their shadow onto the group. Frank Buchman and Russell seem almost to understand Jung's concept of the shadow, but not quite. Part of coming to terms with our shadow is getting past a need to be perfect. We should embrace our shadow rather than "drive in stakes" to protect ourselves from it. We should use the concept to shatter our defenses rather than use it as a defense against those who criticize us. When others criticize us, we should not dismiss their comments by saying that "they are just projecting their shadow onto us," which they may be doing. Rather, we should say, "Maybe they are right." This then opens up reflection upon one's sense of self and possibly a transformation of identity.

But *For Sinners Only* is not about embracing one's dark side. Frank, the miracle worker who is spoken about more than he speaks himself, slowly emerges as a saint, and others seem to achieve beatitude as well. One chapter describes the "ideal home," an entire family of saints. And it was, perhaps, Frank's saintliness that did in the Oxford Group. Frank made some public comments about Hitler (his own shadow?) that led to accusations of his being pro-Nazi. This brought such notoriety onto the group that it adopted a new name, Moral Re-armament, which later evolved into Up with People. But, even with a new name, the movement never quite recovered from Buchman's need to save Hitler—or save himself.

Because of this controversy, AA was reluctant to acknowledge officially its debt to the Oxford Group until the publication of *Alcoholics Anonymous Comes of Age* in 1957. On February 7, 1957, Bill W. wrote to Sam Shoemaker about how he had asked Father Ed Dowling, one of his closest advisors, about how to acknowledge AA's debt to the Oxford Group, given that the pope had once discouraged Catholics from attending Oxford Group meetings. Bill recounted:

> The upshot of an estimate by Father Ed was that full disclosure could do no harm, provided we clearly showed what we had taken from the O.G. and what we had rejected. He felt that A.A. had achieved a public status of its own which would be perfectly capable of taking the revelation of the whole truth. The Church would absorb it too, he thought. Then in his whimsical way he went on to add "After all, the Church does love Aristotle, even if the old boy did believe in abortion!"

The acknowledgment, Bill realized, needed to be made. Certainly, AA adopted a great deal from the Oxford Group. The first AA group in Akron was know as the "alcoholic squadron of the Oxford Group," and early members read widely in Oxford Group literature.[3] They accepted the group's four spiritual activities with little revision (as I will discuss at the end of this chapter). But the group also tried to learn from its mistakes. The Oxford Group was intent on changing the world and so emphasized the importance of recruiting the shakers and movers of society; Bill, without much encouragement from the New York Oxford Group, worked with lowly alcoholics (Kurtz 44–45). AA attempted to avoid associating the movement with a single charismatic leader, and they did not see sainthood as a goal. Nor did they aim to save the world. The rhetoric of AA is directed toward self; the Oxford Group's is often apocalyptic. Consider the following passage from *What Is the Oxford Group?*: "The spirit of the Anti-Christ has reared its head more blatantly in the post–Great War years than ever before. The Anti-Christ spirit is in every walk of life, and enemies of Christ use every means in their power to crush Christianity" (122). And later: "The hour for a Christian Revolution approaches" (131). The members of the Oxford Group saw themselves as saints working for the perfect world.

As C. G. Jung explains in *Modern Man in Search of a Soul,* which Bill W. and Dr. Bob read during the early days of AA, perfection and sainthood are naive and one-sided goals:

> It is painful—there is no denying it—to interpret radiant things from the shadow-side, and thus in a measure reduce them to their origins in dreary filth. But it seems to me to be an imperfection in things of beauty, and a weakness in man, if an explanation from the shadow-side has a destructive effect. The horror which we feel for Freudian interpretations is entirely due to our own barbaric or childish naivete, which believes that there can be heights without corresponding depths, and which blinds us to the really "final" truth that, when carried to extremes, opposites meet. Our mistake would lie in supposing that what is radiant no longer exists because it has been explained from the shadow-side. (41)

Perhaps because he had been reading Jung, Bill W. had great difficulty accepting the Oxford Group's four absolutes (Absolute Honesty, Absolute Purity, Absolute Unselfishness, and Absolute Love); he had trouble accepting any absolutes (Kurtz 46). Absolutes were just another form of alcoholic thinking—what Jung called "one-sided thinking"—as was the quest for perfection.[4] Like Jung, AA strives toward completeness—the incorporation of the shadow, though this specific term is never used in the Big Book—rather than perfection. This is the paragraph from the Big Book that follows the Twelve Steps:

> Many of us exclaimed, "What an order! I can't go through with it." Do not be discouraged. No one among us has been able to maintain anything like perfect adherence to these principles. We are not saints. The point is, that we are willing to grow along spiritual lines. The principles we have set down are guides to progress. We claim spiritual progress rather than spiritual perfection. (60)

This is far closer to Jung than it is to the Oxford Group. While we will never know all of Rowland's story, it was Jung who provided the bridge from his hopeless drinking to his sobriety in the Oxford Group. It was also Jung, perhaps, that allowed Bill W. and Dr. Bob to find some distance from the beliefs of the Oxford Group.

This should not, however, diminish the importance of the Oxford Group to the formation of AA. Its ultimate contribution may have been in creating an environment where a string of cynics—Rowland, Ebby, Bill W., and Dr. Bob—could come to believe. On June 27, 1949, Sam Shoemaker, demonstrating his characteristic humility, wrote to Bill, saying, in effect, that he did not feel he made a significant contribution to the development of AA. Bill W. responded in a July 14, 1949, letter, telling his close friend that he was being "much too generous." But his most eloquent homage to Shoemaker, the Calvary Church, and the Oxford Group came in an April 23, 1963, letter:

> You must remember, Sam, that you were the personification here in New York of all the best that went on in Calvary and in the O.G. of A.A.'s early days. Your impact upon me, and upon some of our other people, was simply immense. So whether the transmission of the Grace occurred by night or by day is quite beside the point. It is also entirely true that the substance of A.A.'s Twelve Steps was derived from the O.G.'s emphasis on the essentials and your unforgettable presentation of this material time after time.
>
> After the alcoholics parted company with the O.G. here in New York, we developed a word-of-mouth program of six steps which was simply a paraphrase of what we had heard and felt at your meetings. The Twelve Steps of A.A. simply represented an attempt to state in more detail, breadth, and depth, what we had been taught—primarily by you. Without this, there could have been nothing—nothing at all.

The Twelve Steps, the core of AA's program, certainly owe a great deal to the Oxford Group's four spiritual activities:

1. The Sharing of our sins and temptations with another Christian life given to God, and to use Sharing as Witness to help others, still unchanged, to recognize and acknowledge their sins.
2. Surrender of our life, past, present, and future, into God's keeping and direction.
3. Restitution to all whom we have wronged directly or indirectly.
4. Listening to, accepting, and relying on God's Guidance and carrying it out in everything we do or say, great or small. *(What Is the Oxford Group?* 8–9)

In the early days, Bill W. and Dr. Bob expanded these four activities to six steps. When he drafted the Big Book, Bill W. expanded them further to the Twelve Steps. Even with the expansions, anyone familiar with the Twelve Steps can see the same developmental path: turning one's life over to God, exploring one's past, making amends, and sharing one's experiences. Yet, we should also acknowledge that AA saw a different goal for this shared path of spiritual development: It encouraged its members to grow toward completeness rather than toward perfection.

3

Coming to Alcoholics Anonymous: Hearing One's Life in the Voices of Others

> The social dimension of AA must not be underestimated, and is probably the single most consequential point of differentiation between AA and other therapies.
> —Edmund B. O'Reilly, *Sobering Tales*

In its first sixty or so years, Alcoholics Anonymous has grown from two members to a worldwide institution—as a grassroots movement and without being highly organized. Because AA has grown piecemeal, local customs abound. Even in a rather small town, alcoholics may have the choice of attending one of many meetings, each with its own rituals and mix of individuals. Nonetheless, it is important for readers, especially those who have never attended an AA meeting and have only a limited knowledge of them from parodic renderings in the mass media, to have some understanding of what typically happens at meetings.[1] It is equally important that readers understand how newcomers work with a sponsor. Storytelling in AA occurs within and draws from a broader cultural context; thus, the talks of AA should be analyzed within context, within an understanding of the relationships that develop during meetings and with a sponsor.

Meetings

While each meeting is different (members often say that they have their favorite meetings, they don't like that meeting, or they feel comfortable at this meeting), a recognizable culture exists (when members travel, they often attend meetings in others cities or countries and comment on how they feel "at home" among strangers). As a general description of meetings, I will discuss a variety of elements that *might* form the setting or certain practices that *might* be ritualized within specific meetings. All of these elements will seldom, if ever, be present at a single meeting, but enough of them are present at most, if not all, meetings to convey a sense of a common culture that transcends regional and national boundaries. These elements will be described from the perspective of a first timer, a person attending his or her first "speaker" meeting. To simplify the discussion, I will refer to the first timer as a woman; the person could, of course, as easily be a man. While the reading of this brief narration of a typical meeting should not be considered a substitute for attending an actual meeting, it should serve to move outsiders—the readers of this book—closer to the position of an insider.

The parking lot. Most likely, she is attending her first meeting because her life has begun to unravel. She might have called the central office, where volunteers answer the phone and direct newcomers to meetings. She may have even had someone come to her home and make what is called a Twelfth Step call, a personal introduction to the program. If so, the member making the call would escort her to the meeting and maybe even serve as a temporary sponsor. If not, she would come to this meeting alone. What she might first notice is the odd mix of cars. Luxury cars are parked next to old pickup trucks, motorcycles next to family cars. She has rarely seen this kind of mix before, except maybe at the mall or a grocery store. As she moves toward the door, a number of members stand in small groups, talking, perhaps smoking as well. Here, she encounters, in unusual clusters, other signs that are usually meant to mark distinctions in class or social groupings. By the clothes, she might make certain assumptions about the professions, the class, or even the hobbies of those standing outside. The tendency to divide into gender alike groups is also less apparent. A man in a business suit stands next to a woman who is obviously a painter; both seem to have come to the meeting straight from work. A woman in an expensive dress, shoes, and accessories chats with a man who seems to be a farmer and a woman who is dressed in shorts and a T-shirt. She might feel a bit uncomfortable at the sight of some of these unofficial "greeters." One seems to be a member of a motorcycle gang. Some simply look "rough." She might also feel left out, like a spouse attending her husband's class reunion. People greet each other with hugs, like they have not seen each other for years. She might hear, "Good to see you." Or "I haven't seen you for a while. I thought you were back out there." Or "There's Bill!" She might feel very off balance. She cannot really get a fix on things. The familiar is juxtaposed with the unfamiliar. She might ask, with some trepidation, if this is where the AA people meet. If so, one of the greeters might introduce himself and escort her into the meeting, where he would introduce her to others, give her some pamphlets, and explain in whispers what is going on in the meeting. Although the first timer moves through the entire meeting (and maybe the next few meetings) in a daze, she begins to feel less uncomfortable.

The room. While the actual meeting place could be any number of possibilities (it might be a room in a church, a meeting room in the back of a restaurant, or a room in an AA club), the first timer might notice a large coffeepot in the back, some books and pamphlets on a table, the Twelve Steps and Twelve Traditions on the wall, maybe even a photograph of Bill W. or Dr. Bob. If it is a room that the group rents and uses exclusively, she might be shocked at its clutter.[2] It might be rather dingy, its walls in need of paint, its furniture old and in need of repair. The first timer would see members greeting each other. There would be a lot of hugging.[3]

The opening. Five or ten minutes after the meeting is supposed to start, the first timer will see one of the members, the chair, step up to the podium and say, "Hello, I'm Bill. I'm an alcoholic." The group will loudly respond, "Hello, Bill." She might already be a little surprised by the levity. She was probably expecting something more like a funeral rather than a party. After all, how could anyone have fun without drinking? Then the chair says, "Let's begin with a moment of silence for the still suffering alcoholic, followed by the serenity prayer." After a few seconds of silence, the crowd recites in unison, "God, grant me the serenity to accept the things I cannot change, the courage to change the things I can, and the wisdom to know the difference." The chair then makes some introductory remarks, allows visitors to introduce themselves by first name only, and then asks a few members to read from the Big Book (usually the beginning of chapter 5, "How It Works," which includes the Twelve Steps). As each person reads, she hears the same introduction and confession ("I'm Sue. I'm an alcoholic") and the same response ("Hello, Sue"). Everyone seems to know each other. Some comments are made about the seventh tradition and the group being self-supporting. A basket is passed, and everyone throws in a dollar. The first timer is probably overwhelmed and does not hear most of this. If she does, she may be confused, a bit dazed. The chair then asks someone to hand out chips. After the same introduction, this person speaks of the significance of the chips, given to members to mark their "birthdays." He says, "The white chip, the color of surrender, symbolizes a willingness to stay sober today. Does anyone want a white chip?" The man who had escorted the first timer in tells her she can accept one, so she walks to the front of the room, her face red, her knees about to buckle, and takes the white chip. The man at the front of the room gives her a white chip and a hug. As she walks back to her chair, several other members stand to give her a hug. She feels embarrassed but also good about being accepted and even a little proud about making this first commitment.

The speaker. Someone stands up, goes through the ritual introduction and response, and then begins to introduce the speaker. The first timer has trouble following it all, but there are a lot of comments about the times they spent together, how the speaker had helped him out, maybe a few funny anecdotes. Then the speaker rises and hugs the person who introduced him and begins to talk. The first timer hears only bits, but she might be surprised by the honesty. The speaker may talk about stealing, attempting suicide, having affairs, or letting others down. The confessions may be made with tears or with little emotion. The audience seems very responsive, nodding from time to time, perhaps crying. Despite the wild range of emotions that the speaker takes the audience through, there is also humor. The first timer expected the tears, but not the laughter. When the speaker finishes, there is a standing ovation and more hugs, so many hugs. The first timer may be ambivalent about so much expression of emotion. She might want to be cynical and say that it is all phony. She might feel that she is the one person who does not belong here. But she also wants to be a member, to have this many friends, and to have the sense of peace that the speaker exhibited.

The closing. The chair again comes to the podium and says a few words. The first timer is hearing little of what is being said. She might later describe this experience as feeling like she was in a fishbowl, hearing only muffled sounds. The chair then says, "Will all who care to join in the Lord's Prayer." The first timer doesn't know how to react to all of the talk about prayer and one's higher power. "All of the members stand, join hands in one large circle, bow their heads, and recite the Lord's Prayer. Then they look up and recite, "Keep coming back. It works." All around the room, people turn and give each other hugs. Someone turns to the first timer and says, "Would you like a hug?" She nods her head, and they hug.

The aftermath. Several people stay after to talk to the first timer. Someone might even take her out for coffee or ask her to come with a group to a restaurant. Phone numbers are often shared. The first timer is surprised that some people begin to call her almost every day, asking her how she is doing, inviting her to meetings. She begins to attend other meetings at other times and other locations. Some are "Big Book study" meetings, where someone reads a passage from the Big Book and everyone takes a turn commenting on it. Some are step meetings, where members discuss how they are working one of the Twelve Steps. Some are topic meetings, where someone raises a topic (e.g., relapse, letting go, gratitude, faith), and then others comment on it. She soon has a sponsor and is meeting with her once a week or so to work the steps. When she has a bad day, she makes a phone call and people begin to show up at her house. She finds that she can always call someone, even in the middle of the night.

The first timer is surprised by how quickly she meets people, how soon she feels a part of the group. Within a few weeks, she may be chairing a session, handing out chips, or escorting in other first timers.

Sponsorship

The most important interaction outside of meetings is sponsorship. Newcomers are advised to find a sponsor as soon as possible, although some may take several years to make this commitment. Alcoholics usually describe themselves as people who like to be in control. The idea of turning their will over to God and allowing themselves to be directed by a sponsor is difficult. Danny says, "I keep remembering my reluctance to get a sponsor, because I didn't want somebody telling me what to do" (T., *A Sponsorship Guide* 54). Certainly, many newcomers feel like they are being "bossed around."[4]

Sponsors become mentors for newcomers, introducing them to the program and starting them on the process of "working the steps." The sponsor may ask the sponsee to "check in" every day, attend a meeting every day, ask for three phone numbers at every meeting, read certain chapters in the Big Book, and/or begin writing about the steps, starting with Step One. For example, the sponsor might ask the sponsee to take Step One ("We admitted we were powerless over alcohol—that our lives had become unmanageable") and write several pages (maybe only one, maybe as many as twenty) on the key words (say, "powerless" and "unmanageable"). The sponsor might even ask the sponsee to rewrite the assignment until it seems like he or she is coming to some basic understanding of it.

Most importantly, the sponsor is the person who forces the newcomer to cut through all of that "alcoholic bullshit." The sponsor, as fellow alcoholic, is able to recognize certain patterns of thinking that might lead to a relapse and challenge them. One often hears, "You can't bullshit a bullshitter." Ray O'K. humorously describes his first encounter with his sponsor, after he had been attending meetings off and on for a few years, in this way:

> I told him what was going on with me and he said he'd be right over. And he came in. And he looked so good, and I felt so bad. And I said, "What should I do, John?" He gave me that look, you know that look that sponsors have. And he said, "Don't drink and go to meetings. You'll be all right." Well, I didn't want him to tell me that! And I told him I didn't want him to tell me that. I said, "John, I'm a smart guy, tell me something else." And he just gave me a look and said, "Don't drink and go to meetings." I said, "John, you really don't understand the problem. The problem is I shouldn't be working in a place like this. I'm too good of a lawyer to be in this dump." And

he said, "Yea, that's probably true. Well, if you don't drink and you go to meetings, maybe things will get better." I said, "Home is worse. I'm not even supposed to go up there." And he said, "If you don't drink and go to meetings . . ." I said, "I'm being sued by a bank for money. There was a misunderstanding about a loan application." He said, "Yea, I think I heard about that one. Well, if you don't drink and go to meetings . . ." You know, I sensed that there was no dialogue there. He didn't even know that I was from a dysfunctional family. God sends us the right sponsor, does he not? (AA Talk)

As the audience laughs at the sponsor's simple solution to Ray's complex problems, they acknowledge that they once thought as Ray does (their problems seemed too complex to solve) and that their sponsors gave them similarly simple answers (don't drink, go to meetings, work the steps, read the Big Book).

While this relationship might seem, at first glance, like the most hierarchical structure in AA, it is actually rather dialogic—despite Ray's joke that there is no dialogue in the relationship. Sponsors have their own sponsors (O'Reilly, *Sobering Tales* 135). They do not "graduate" to being on their own; nor do they come to a point where they assume they have nothing else to learn. As Mariasha says, "To think you've arrived and no longer need to check out reality with another human being is a dangerous position to take" (T., *A Sponsorship Guide* 8).

It is also the nature of the sponsor/sponsee relationship to invert social norms. In his story, Ken D. speaks of an old-timer and his relationship with his sponsees:

I always liked Lewis because he lived in a trailer that was like a silver bullet, I don't even know what they call it. And these guys would come over from La Hoya, living in three and four million dollar homes and driving brand new cars and they would go up to Lewis and say, "Lewis, I need your help. It's not working." And Lewis would come out of this trailer and he would bring folding chairs, cause he would never let you in the trailer, no room, and he'd sit there and just visit with you. And then send you off by saying, "Don't worry. You're going to be okay." (AA Talk)

In our culture, we would expect Lewis to ask for advice from the men living in $3 million and $4 million homes, but we would not expect them to seek out Lewis.

The dialogic nature of sponsorship—and its tendency to invert norms —aids in the prevention of a common problem associated with confession within the context of psychotherapy. Jung writes:

Let us suppose that in a given case the confession demanded by the method of catharsis has taken place—that the neurosis has disappeared, or that the symptoms at least have vanished. The patient

> could now be dismissed as cured if it depended on the physician alone. But he—or especially she—cannot get away. The patient seems bound to the physician by the act of confession. If this apparently meaningless attachment is forcibly severed, there is a bad relapse. (*Modern Man in Search of a Soul* 37)

Jung is writing of the problem of transference. As secrets separate us, confession draws us together. When the patient confesses and the therapist does not, transference often develops. The sense of freedom emerging from confession is undercut by a fixation—and perhaps a dependence—on the therapist. But, as is the case in AA, if sponsees confess to their sponsors but also witness their sponsors confess at a topic meeting or speaker meeting, then transference is far less likely to occur.

Also indicative of the dialogic nature of the relationship, sponsors also often speak of learning from their sponsees. Marge says:

> I have learned an incredible amount by experiencing the processes of my sponsees. A lot of them have made faster progress than I ever made, especially emotionally, because they have the emotional equipment when they get sober. I didn't. And they have the willingness that I didn't have. I learned a tremendous amount from their serenity, directness, and honesty. (T., *A Sponsorship Guide* 55)

As Ed explains, sponsors often feel that helping a sponsee is actually what makes the program work for them: "A sponsee gives me the chance to take everything I've learned in the rooms, mix it up with my life experiences, and then serve it up in such a way that I feel reborn. *I come to believe all over again.* My sponsees keep me clean" (60). In the early days of AA, the distinction between sponsors and sponsees was even more blurred. Newcomers frequently and of necessity became sponsors rather quickly, perhaps when they had only a few months or a few weeks of sobriety. But it is still not unusual for someone with six months in the program to become a sponsor or someone with a year of sobriety to become a sponsor for someone with three years.

The sponsor/sponsee relationship is typically described as being rather intense, marked by a high degree of honesty and trust (a sponsee shares with a sponsor what is too private to speak about at meetings), but the relationship is difficult to define. The Big Book does not mention sponsorship at all, because it is part of the program lore that was being developed in Cleveland (primarily through the work of Clarence, one of the early members of AA) about the time the Big Book was being written. No sanctioned guidelines for being a sponsor exist. Mariasha says:

> The most healing thing my sponsor has ever said to me is there aren't any rules, except that you can't use and be in my house. Whenever I've called her with any kind of self-reproach for not doing what I

> should be doing, or could be doing, or not meeting any expectations
> with her, whether they be mine or hers, she has always comforted
> me and said, "I don't have any expectations of you; I'm here to sup-
> port you; you call me as often as you need to, or you feel you want
> to. But, I don't need anything more from you than for you to utilize
> me at whatever pace you feel comfortable." I think that's been the
> most important thing for me and what I pass on, that being spon-
> sored should not be a pressure. She has never put any kind of pres-
> sure or burden on me. (T., *A Sponsorship Guide* 24)

Mariasha's relationship to her sponsor makes it sound like it is always
founded on what is commonly called "unconditional love." But that is
not always the case. Some sponsors take an approach that is more like
what is often called "tough love." Jeanette says of her expectations of
sponsees: "They must be willing to go through the steps, along with a
commitment to stay clean. Otherwise, I wouldn't give two cents for the
way they feel" (59). Ken D. says of his sponsor:

> And my sponsor, I hear people say, "Your sponsor is loving and
> kind." Yea. And I would call him up and complain about everything
> and he would listen for two or three minutes and then he'd say, "Hey
> Ken, maybe you'll get lucky and die tonight." And then he'd hang
> up. It was like, where is this warmth? If you don't have a sponsor,
> you should get one so you can learn all of those dirty tricks to pull
> on someone else. (AA Talk)

In ordinary circumstances with people outside of the program, this kind
of response would be considered insensitive and harsh. Yet, it was just
what Ken needed to hear to move out of his self-pity, as he acknowledges
with his humor. While members of AA are encouraged to feel, maybe for
the first time consciously, a number of emotions (especially fear, which
the program views as being the basis for other emotions like anger or
resentment), some emotions (especially, self-pity and self-righteous anger) are not often tolerated. Ken D.'s sponsor would not have reacted in
the same way if Ken had called and said something like, "I'm afraid of
starting this new job." Or "A close friend just died." However, even once
we recognize the sponsor's attempt to move Ken D. past self-pity, the
response is not the kind of exchange that we would typically tolerate (or
benefit from) in other kinds of relationships. It would be considered
unprofessional for a therapist to say, "Maybe you'll get lucky and die,"
and then hang up. Most of us would not tolerate this kind of brusque
challenge from a friend. We expect a friend to commiserate with us, re-
assure us in our belief that the world is against us or that we have every
right to be angry. It is precisely this kind of response, or other forms of
honesty, that is fairly common between sponsor and sponsee, although

many sponsors have a far more nurturing style of challenging sponsees than Ken's sponsor.

The relationship between sponsor and sponsee is—like the rituals of meetings—highly variable. Some sponsors ask their sponsees to call them every day; others simply say, "Call me when you need to." Some require extensive writing on the steps; others talk to their sponsees about what the steps mean. Some give specific directives (e.g., attend a meeting every day); others allow their sponsees to work out their own approaches to the program. So, part of finding one's way in the program is finding the right sponsor. Newcomers might find and "fire" several sponsors before they develop an intense and lasting relationship. Even old-timers may switch sponsors every few years as a means of learning a new perspective on the program or making a fresh start at the steps. While the switching of sponsors causes some hurt feelings, it is typically considered a rather ordinary occurrence. Even as they are in the early stages of building rapport, some sponsors ask their sponsees, "Just tell me when I'm fired."

4

Ritualized Reading: The Voices In and Around Sacred Texts

> Cybernetics, information theory, statistics, and the problem
> of the text. The problem of incarnating the text. The bound-
> aries of this incarnation.
>
> A human act is a potential text and can be understood (as
> a human act and not a physical motion) only in the dialogic
> context of its time (as a rejoinder, as a semantic position, as a
> system of motives).
>
> —M. M. Bakhtin, "The Problem of the Text"

Members of AA are avid readers of program literature. Indeed, reading about the program becomes, for many newcomers, an obsession that ameliorates, if only partially, the obsession to drink. And so understanding the sacred texts of the program—how they are ritualized and
incarnated—is crucial to understanding what happens in meetings and
between meetings. In this chapter, I will discuss the central texts of AA
and say something about the rituals that surround the use of these texts.

Alcoholics Anonymous: The Story of How Many Thousands of Men and Women Have Recovered from Alcoholism

Alcoholics Anonymous is the most important text in the program.[1] When
it was nearing production, Bill W. chose the thickest paper available "to
convince the alcoholic purchaser that he was indeed getting his money's
worth" (*'Pass It On'* 205). The bulk of the volume earned it the nick-
name of the Big Book.[2]

Most of the text was drafted by Bill W.—actually dictated to his secretary—and then reviewed by Dr. Bob (who disliked any form of writing, even correspondence) and other early AA members. Although Dr.
Bob did not draft the manuscript, it is generally accepted that he is re-

sponsible for many of the ideas in the Big Book. In his last talk before an AA conference, Dr. Bob recounted:

> I didn't write the Twelve Steps. I had nothing to do with the writing of them. I think probably I had something to do with them indirectly because, after the June 10th episode, Bill came to live at our house and stayed for about three months. And there was hardly a night in that three months that we didn't stay up until two or three o'clock discussing these things. And it would be hard for me to conceive that something wasn't said during those nightly discussions around our kitchen table that influenced the writing of the Twelve Steps. They are much more handy in that form. Of course, we had the ideas pretty much, basically, if not in that terse and fanciful form. (AA Talk)

The Big Book should certainly be viewed as a collaboration among the early members, including Dr. Bob, his wife Anne, Bill W.'s wife Lois, and others. In a 1960 talk, Bill W. said that the feedback he received from Dr. Bob and others was overwhelming, that he felt like he was "getting it from all sides."

Some members of AA argue that the Big Book was inspired by some higher power. Whether a work of collaboration or inspiration, Bill W., its author in the most restricted sense of the term, certainly grew into its spiritual message. On March 25, 1940, Bill W. wrote to Ted:

> I explained this at some length because I want you to be successful with yourself and people with whom you work. We used to pussy-foot on the spiritual business a great deal out there and the result was bad, for our record falls quite a lot short of the performance of Akron and Cleveland where there are now about 350 alcoholics, many of them sober two or three years, with less than 20% ever having had any relapse. Out there they have always emphasized the spiritual way of life as the core of our procedure, and we have begun to follow suit in New York for the simple reason that our record was only half as good, most of the difference being directly attributable to temporizing over what it really takes to fix the drunks. Doctors not closely acquainted with us naturally believed that this thing would work just as well on the moral psychology business. On the other hand, physicians are men with the scientific spirit, and are usually convinced by facts and percentages which we certainly now have.

Here, Bill W. seems to have only recently come to an appreciation of the spiritual message that he drafted about two years earlier, which suggests that others—Dr. Bob and his wife Anne, Bill's wife Lois, early members, Sam Shoemaker, and perhaps others—significantly influenced the content of the Big Book.

In the above letter, Bill W. seems to be moving toward an acceptance of the spiritual message of the Big Book because he has been convinced by "facts and percentages," that is, the success of the Akron group. Later, in a May 14, 1957, letter to John F., he is more clearly motivated by the spiritual:

> Therefore, John, I have long since laid aside any pretensions to having received a miraculous and calculated intervention of God in the sense that St. Paul receive [*sic*] his. Maybe I did, but I certainly have no affirmative conviction about it. In fact, I prefer not to have any such conviction, least it unloose my pride once more. It would be utterly presumptuous for me to try to judge of such a matter. Perhaps it is natural for many people to assume, on account of the large reach and power of A.A. today, that God did make a very special intervention in my case. But I certainly must not assume this, and hope I shall never again be tempted. To make A.A. possible, God's leaven had to work through a great many people. The mainstreams of influence can be traced back through Carl Jung, high Episcopalian Sam Shoemaker, and thence back to the church itself.

I raise this issue to support an earlier point: When Bill W. *wrote* his story for the Big Book, he was still early in his recovery. It took him decades to grow into the spiritual message of the book, and so the way that he tells his story there may not reflect the spiritual maturity of many old-timers that one might hear at local meetings.

As I argued earlier, the stories in the Big Book, as texts written and edited for print, fail to capture the oral tradition of storytelling in the program. The importance of the oral tradition is also marked by the fact that early members were not very enthusiastic about writing down their program in *Alcoholics Anonymous*. At least one early member of AA was so upset about the prospect of a book about the program that he used it as an excuse to get drunk; reportedly, he thought that "Doc and Bill were going to make a fortune, and he wanted his share" (*Dr. Bob* 153). Certainly, Bill W. had to work rather hard to sell the idea ('*Pass It On*' 190). Once the project was underway, Jim S., a journalist and early member, interviewed individual members from the Akron area and helped them write their stories, editing final versions. Reportedly, the New York members drafted their own stories, which were then heavily edited by Bill W. and Hank P., sometimes contrary to the wishes of the authors ('*Pass It On*' 200). The stories were edited to accent "different phases of the drinkers' common experience"—so that alcoholics would not read the stories and feel that they were different (Kurtz 73)—and to challenge the stereotype of the alcoholic as a "Skid-Row bum" (74).

The first 164 pages contain Bill W.'s story, with an outline of the program and how it works; the volume is completed with examples of members telling their stories. The third edition of the Big Book contains forty-three stories, including Bill W.'s.

Members consider the book to be a spiritual document, and selections are typically read and ritualized at meetings. One such section is known as "The Promises":

> If we are painstaking about this phase of our development, we will be amazed before we are half way through. We are going to know a new freedom and a new happiness. We will not regret the past nor wish to shut the door on it. We will comprehend the word serenity and we will know peace. No matter how far down the scale we have gone, we will see how our experience can benefit others. That feeling of uselessness and self-pity will disappear. We will lose interest in selfish things and gain interest in our fellows. Self-seeking will slip away. Our whole attitude and outlook upon life will change. Fear of people and of economic insecurity will leave us. We will intuitively know how to handle situations which used to baffle us. We will suddenly realize that God is doing for us what we could not do for ourselves.
>
> Are these extravagant promises? We think not. They are being fulfilled among us—sometimes quickly, sometimes slowly. They will always materialize if we work for them. (83–84)

When such passages are communally read or recited from memory at meetings and then interpreted, usually by applying the insight to the speaker's life, the printed words are drawn into the orality of the meeting and so take on the values of the culture. As I suggested in chapter 1, the culture of AA can hardly be understood by reading the Big Book apart from its ritualized practice and its oral hermeneutic tradition. Learning to interpret the text within its oral tradition is an important means of "reworking the self." In "Oral Genres and the Art of Reading in Tibet," Anne Carolyn Klein discusses the oral forms of interpretation followed by Tibetan Buddhists. She argues that Western practices of reading can hardly convey the range of cultural practices in the Tibetan culture:

> [T]he modern secular construct of "reading" seems inadequate to describe Tibetan textual engagement. The face-to-face and often ritualized encounter with the person whose oral commentary is integral to the experience of text is one differentiating factor; another and even more significant difference is what occurs through repeated practice of the text, that is, through performing the procedures it reaches, including recitation, visualization, and conceptual training. One is not so much reworking the written text—although this is a crucial and fundamental practice in many quarters—as reworking the self. Nor does the usual meaning of "reading" illuminate the nonconceptual processes of calming, breathing, concentration, and mental intensity so central to meditative textual practices. (309)

In Big Book study meetings, one can see instruction—a "face-to-face" ritualization—on the reading of this text at work. The truth in the Big Book might seem "ready-made" and monologic. However, within the context of meetings, only brief passages are read, and they are then commented on by virtually every person in the room. The normative power of the unchanging printed word is not given greater meaning than how it applies to the lives of those discussing it. Meaning emerges, in Bakhtin's words, "*between people* collectively searching for truth, in the process of their dialogic interaction" (*Problems of Dostoevsky's Poetics* 110). Newcomers might think, for example, that "The Promises" guarantee an ideal life within the program, but old-timers will quickly assert that its promises are, indeed, not "extravagant" but realistic and achievable. The Big Book does not promise riches; rather, it promises freedom from "fear of economic instability." It does not promise a life without problems; rather, it promises that solutions to problems will come "intuitively." Within the communal hermeneutic, one comes to understand how the group thinks (they are brought into a dialogue that has been evolving since 1935), yet individuals are allowed to voice their unique slant on the text. Because the meaning of the text comes from the voices in the room, the sense is that "truth" is not in the text; rather, "truth" emerges during each meeting.

Even though the reading of passages like "The Promises" is often routinely performed at meetings while those who have heard the passage read hundreds of times chat among themselves, the impact of the text is sometimes profoundly felt. After a long introduction by Carol, Carolyn N. began to share an experience from her early days in the program:

> Hearing Carol up here laughing reminds me of real early in sobriety, I was right here at this meeting on a Friday night and they asked me to read "The Promises." I was more than happy to get up and read "The Promises," but the only trouble was when I started reading "The Promises," it really made me sad because, you know, I just thought those promises would never, ever come true for me. And, um, so . . . and I was going through a really hard time. It was really hard for me to be sober, because I hadn't been sober in a good many years. And, when I started reading these promises, and there were more people in the room than tonight, and I just started crying, and I couldn't stop. And I thought, "Oh, God, I've got to stop crying." But I couldn't stop crying. The only way I could stop crying, and you all were very patient, just like you were with Carol, was to look up at your faces. You sat here and you watched me cry. First, I thought, "I'll leave." Because that's what I always do when things get going tough. I cut my losses, and I'm out of there. But I thought, "No, no, these are my fellow alcoholics and all my friends," and so I looked up and looked into your faces and you all were still there and I could finish reading. But, um, so that's something that has always stuck with me. (AA Talk)

This kind of response, which is fairly common, represents but one way that the meaning of the text is embodied as it is spoken by one person standing before others, as the audience witnesses its bodily effect on the person reading the text. In this way, newcomers can bring a section of the Big Book back to life for old-timers who might otherwise lose touch with their early days of sobriety. The text emerges as a powerful force as members interpret it through their own life experiences, through, we might even say, their collective life experience. It is not a text that is interpreted through other texts or experiences outside of what it means to live as an alcoholic. In his study of the reading strategies of Jewish reading groups on the Lower East Side of New York, Boyarin comments on the need for this "closed" group to "free" themselves from "influences" so that they could "properly receive the Torah" ("Voices Around the Text" 224). Although it is never directly stated, AA members model and acknowledge the interpretation of the Big Book from life experience. The attempt to interpret this text through other texts (psychology, anthropology, history, etc.) is rather rare, and while this practice is not directly criticized, it is not warmly received.

In AA, as I will discuss in more detail later, all ideas seem open to critique and parody, even sacred texts like the Big Book (Flynn 93–94). I have heard more than one member comment on how, when still a newcomer, he or she suggested that the Big Book should be updated; some even add that they would be willing to take a shot at it. This is roughly akin to an ordinary person, recently converted to Christianity, suggesting that he or she should be allowed to revise the Bible.[3] Such revisions are not really needed, however, because the text is interpreted and reinterpreted within an evolving communal hermeneutic. When members wrote to Bill W. and asked for his interpretation of some passage of the Big Book, he was reluctant to answer as an authority. Bill W.'s May 14, 1957, letter to John F. about the word "God" in *Alcoholics Anonymous Comes of Age* illustrates his willingness to open the interpretation of all AA literature:

> You'll remember there was another spot in the manuscript where the Buddhists wanted to substitute the word "Good" for "God" in the Twelve Steps. Here I felt I could make only a partial accommodation. To begin with, the Steps are not enforceable upon anyone—they are only suggestions. A belief in the Steps or God is not in any way a requisite for A.A. membership. Therefore we have no means of compelling anyone to stay away from AA because he does not believe in God or the Twelve Steps. In fact A.A. has a technique of reducing rebellion among doubting people by deliberately inviting them to disagree with everything we believe in. We merely suggest that the doubters stick around and get acquainted. They are assured

they are members if they say so. In truth, many an agnostic and atheist newcomer, including some fallen away Catholics, have substituted the word "Good" for "God" in the Twelve Steps. By practicing the program with "Good" in mind, they almost invariably come back to the same kind of concept of God—usually a personal God. Whether this will happen to our Buddhist members, I don't know. But it certainly can't make the least difference to any of us what the Buddhists do with the Steps. The Steps are for everybody to take or leave alone as they wish, in whole or in part. Had we not taken this attitude it is possible that thousands who are today believing and A.A. members, and often good Church members, would never have joined us at all. They would have been dead ducks by now.

It is through a communal and open hermeneutic that the fellowship of AA continually renews its texts.

Daily Meditation Books

From the Oxford Group, AA inherited the practice of beginning the day with a time of prayer, meditation, and reading of spiritual texts. During this time, members typically read from a book of daily meditations that presents some aspect of the AA ideology and suggests a topic for further thought or a task for the day. A passage from *Twenty-Four Hours a Day* reads:

Oct. 7—A.A. Thought for the Day
Do I put too much reliance on any one member of the group? That is, do I make a tin god out of some one person? Do I set that person on a pedestal? If I do, I am building my house on sand. All A.A. members have "clay feet." They are all only one drink away from a drunk, no matter how long they have been in A.A. This has been proved to be true more than once. It's not fair to any member to be singled out as a leader in A.A. and to always quote that member on the A.A. program. If that person should fail, where would I be? *Can I afford to be tipped over by the failure of my ideal?*

Meditation for the Day
You must always remember that you are weak but that God is strong. God knows all about your weakness. He hears every cry for mercy, every sign of weakness, every plea for help, every sorrow over failure, every weakness felt and expressed. We only fail when we trust too much to our own strength. Do not feel bad about your weakness. When you are weak, that is when God is strong to help you. Trust God enough, and your weakness will not matter. God is always strong to save.

Prayer for the Day
I pray that I may learn to lean on God's strength. I pray that I may know that my weakness is God's opportunity.

Members usually have one or several of these books that direct their morning spiritual time. They sometimes write marginalia, comments heard during meetings, insights, or dated descriptions of the problems they face today; these words are then reread, almost as a gage of their progress in the program, as they cycle their way through the book each year.

Ancillary Texts

Members also read a wide range of books on the history of the program (*Alcoholics Anonymous Comes of Age, Dr. Bob and the Good Oldtimers, 'Pass It On'*, Kurtz's *Not-God*, etc.) as well as books that the founders and early members read (James's *The Varieties of Religious Experience*, Jung's *Modern Man in Search of a Soul*, etc.). All of these works have a spiritual—yet not a strictly religious—focus. One of the most widely read and admired is Emmet Fox's *The Sermon on the Mount*. One passage reads:

> Now we can choose the sort of thoughts that we entertain. It will be a little difficult to break a bad habit of thought, but it can be done. We can choose how we shall think—in point of fact, we always do choose—and therefore our lives are just the result of the kind of thoughts we have chose to hold; and therefore they are of our own ordering; and therefore there is perfect justice in the universe. No suffering for another man's original sin, but the reaping of a harvest that we ourselves have sown. We have free will, but our free will lies in our choice of thought. (14)

Books like *The Sermon on the Mount* provide a way of knowing the mind set of the founders and the early members, a way of knowing their way of working the program and emerging from a dark period of drinking. Fox's passage expresses one of the central ideas of the program: We cannot change other people or control the events in our lives, but we can change how we think about them, and it is through changing our way of thinking that we achieve serenity. Even though local groups form their own rituals and their own local wisdom, this basic idea can be heard in meetings across the country and around the world. Such core beliefs are not handed down from a central office; rather, they emerge as diverse individuals find value in the same passages from the same texts.

5

The Twelve Steps: Finding One's Voice among the Other Voices

> When I first came to AA and I started taking the Steps, that
> was my salvation because up until that time, I didn't realize
> it, but I was living under an assumed identity in a delusional
> state. And when I started going through the Steps, the Steps
> evicted me from my hiding places. They threw me out. They
> said, "You can't have these props anymore, because that's
> make believe. If you are going to stay here and stay sober,
> you're going to have to deal with reality."
>
> —Ken D., AA Talk

> The utterance is filled with *dialogic overtones,* and they must
> be taken into account in order to understand fully the style
> of the utterance.
>
> —M. M. Bakhtin, "The Problem of Speech Genres"

The Twelve Steps form the *suggested* path of development for the individual; they are usually "worked" with one's sponsor. Newcomers often express a great deal of confidence about their ability to work
through the steps in rather quick order; they think of it as a rather simple
process that is worked once. Old-timers tend to think of the steps as a
guide to living. Working them is a slow, never-ending process. Bill W.
himself acknowledged this in a July 27, 1953, letter to Sam Shoemaker
on the occasion of the publication of the *Twelve Steps and the Twelve
Traditions*:

> Am sending you a copy of A.A.'s newest book, dealing with our
> Twelve Steps and Twelve Traditions. Seemingly, this is a prescription
> for our whole Society and all the individuals in it. Being nearly all
> exposition, it's rather pedestrian and I think it pontificates too much.
> I know [sic] understand why—I think I was trying to write a pre-
> scription for myself. The Tradition part—nearly all of it heavily de-

flationary to me personally—I think I have accepted in full. But when it comes to the deep implications of the Twelve Steps—well, that's something else again!

Bill, writing here some eighteen years after codifying the steps, was still struggling to understand them and work them.

While I will not write at length on the steps here, a rudimentary understanding of them is crucial to the analysis of the program's storytelling, as presented in later chapters. The comments in this chapter, thus, should not be regarded as an "official" interpretation; my purpose is to present the steps primarily as they relate to the structure and content of AA talks, not so much as they are used as a path of spiritual growth. As I discuss the steps, I will group them into three categories that relate to the three-part structure of AA talks: how we were (or the drunkolog), what happened (or how we came to AA), and how we are now (as recovering alcoholics in AA). The steps, thus, inform much of the structure—and, one might add, content—of AA stories. Further, it is by working the steps that one develops a "voice" that is unique yet clearly situated within the ethos of the program. Bakhtin writes:

> In each epoch, in each social circle, in each small world of family, friends, acquaintances, and comrades in which a human being grows and lives, there are always authoritative utterances that set the tone— artistic, scientific, and journalistic works on which one relies, to which one refers, which are cited, imitated, and followed. In each epoch, in all areas of life and activity, there are particular traditions that are expressed and retained in verbal vestments: in written words, in utterances, in sayings, and so forth. . . .
>
> This is why the unique speech experience of each individual is shaped and developed in continuous and constant interaction with others' individual utterances. This experience can be characterized to some degree as the process of *assimilation*—more or less creative— of others' words. . . . ("Problem of Speech Genres" 88–89)

Style (one's voice) is, Bakhtin suggests, a process of assimilation, which includes knowing "the authoritative utterances that set the tone" (what I earlier called *sacred texts*) and taking "others' words" (which have "their own evaluative tone") and making them part of our text (or utterance) as we "rework, re-accentuate" them. Within AA, speakers develop a style (or voice) by assimilating to models like Bill W.'s story (as well as the other stories in the Big Book and the stories of old-timers that they hear firsthand at meetings) and by learning the program (typically by working the steps in meetings or with one's sponsor). All speakers incorporate the words of others in their stories, which would make it seem that there is only one style and one story. To some extent this is true. I have heard members say that they usually know when they are around someone who is in a twelve-step program just by how they talk. But each story is also different. As the speaker says the words of others, he or she "re-accentuates" them. It is with this revaluation of the "others' words" that each story becomes unique.

The first three steps ask newcomers to admit that they are powerless and then surrender control to *their* higher power. Alcoholics, who have always been told that they needed more willpower, are now told that they are too willful:

1. We admitted we were powerless over alcohol—that our lives had become unmanageable.
2. Came to believe that a Power greater than ourselves could restore us to sanity.
3. Made a decision to turn our will and our lives over to the care of God *as we understood Him.*

The subject of the steps is the plural "we," which is less preachy, emphasizing the importance of working the steps within a group, and its actions are expressed in the past tense, which emphasizes that this is the plan others have already followed and found effective in achieving sobriety.[1]

The first three steps relate to the first section of AA talks, which deals with the way that speakers were, or the drunkolog. The progression of the disease, a growing sense that their lives are unraveling, leads to the acceptance of these steps. Indeed, many speakers comment on how they had already accepted the first three steps by the time that they walked into their first AA meeting.

With these early steps, newcomers come to recognize the AA distinction between spirituality and religion. Many newcomers, atheists or agnostics, express concern about accepting any notion of a higher power.[2] Those who are already religious may have problems with the notion that they can, in effect, choose the God they will believe in. AA affirms a need to be close to a higher power, even as it argues against the kind of dogma that many, especially those who have renounced the training of their childhoods, associate with organized religion. While this distinction between spirituality and religion might seem highly critical of organized religion, I have never had any sense that members, even those who are intensely involved with organized religion, are offended by it. I think what is typically meant by the expression ("AA is about spirituality and not religion") does not preclude the possibility of developing one's spirituality within organized religion; rather, it suggests that spirituality is more than simply attending church.

The first three steps—indeed, all of the steps—are frequently discussed during step meetings and even during speaker meetings. The following, from Dick M.'s story, shows how the text of the steps are interpreted within the community and how working the steps becomes part of the content of stories. Dick M. is speaking of his difficulty understanding the third step:

> There were some guys talking out there, and I run right up there in the middle of them, and one was Charlie P. and one was Wayne P. and one was Neil L. They was sitting there having their conversation so I said, "I don't mean to bother you boys but there's something I got to know." I said, "I'm having a hell of a time with the Third Step of AA. Somebody's got to tell me how to go about doing this. And I've read the book, but how do you turn your will and life over to the care of God?" Charlie didn't have too much to say. He just said, "Let me ask you one question." Said, "Can you make a decision?" I said, "Hell yea, I can make a decision. Not long ago, I was making one every morning. In fact, sometimes I had to make two, quick. Because I'd get up, sit on the side of the bed, and light me a cigarette, and then I'd jump up and head for the bathroom and I'd have to decide whether I was goin' to put my head or my ass on that commode." Charlie said, "That's a decision. And the first thing you got to do is do that. You've got your work cut out for you once you've made that decision. Because you've got all them other Steps down through there. But first thing you've got to do is make a decision. Can you make a decision?" You know, I ain't had no more problems with the Third Step. (AA Talk)

This anecdote suggests something of the communal interpretive process that surrounds the steps. When a newcomer is making the steps too cryptic or onerous, an old-timer will simplify them. When a newcomer claims to have mastered the steps, an old-timer will, in some way, suggest that they are too complex and difficult to have mastered so quickly. For example, when one newcomer claimed to have worked all of the steps in two weeks, an old-timer responded, "Keep coming back." In other words, "You may think you have it, but you aren't even close." What the community attempts to achieve is a fluidity of interpretation that keeps newcomers (and old-timers, for that matter) moving through the steps, reinterpreting them, and finding new ways to apply them to their lives. Frequently, one hears even an old-timer say, "I'm back at Step One." Or "I feel, after two years in the program, like I have just taken Step One."

The passage from Dick M.'s talk also illustrates the dialogic nature of AA and AA stories. With the transcript above, the voices are marked by quotation marks; on the audiotape, from which I transcribed this section, the voices are marked by shifts in Dick's intonation. In a rather short segment of this talk, we hear the voice of Dick M., who narrates the encounter, but we also hear the voice of Dick's former self and the voice of Charlie, the old-timer who sets Dick straight. What is difficult to convey in print is how Dick's intonation (or his re-accentuation of the "others' words") not only constructs *his* voice but also preserves traces of his development within the program. We hear Dick parody himself as newcomer (speaking of how he struggled to understand the third step), and we hear Dick the newcomer parody himself as practicing alcoholic (trying to decide whether he was going to put his "head" or his "ass on that commode"); we hear Dick revere the voice of Charlie (one of the voices that Dick will assimilate) and the voice of Dick as he is now (the narrative voice of the entire anecdote, a voice that has become more like the voice of Charlie). It is, as Bakhtin says, by taking the words of others and giving them a new intonation that Dick finds his place in the program and his voice as an AA speaker.

The next six steps—which relate to the "what happened" portion of AA talks, or how members began to work the program—ask them to move backward, assess their moral character, and make amends. This portion of the steps allows alcoholics to come to terms with their past, as preparation for spiritual growth:

4. Made a searching and fearless moral inventory of ourselves.
5. Admitted to God, to ourselves, and to another human being the exact nature of our wrongs.
6. Were entirely ready to have God remove all these defects of character.
7. Humbly asked Him to remove our shortcomings.
8. Made a list of all persons we had harmed, and became willing to make amends to them all.
9. Made direct amends to such people wherever possible, except when to do so would injure them or others.

While this process would seem to be a task tackled once in an adult's life, many members speak of having to go through the process several times before they feel that they are able to be completely honest. Those who work these steps describe feeling a great sense of relief. They also speak of it as a humbling experience. As one member said, "If you get to the Ninth Step and you still have any ego left, you haven't done it right."

Of all the steps, the fourth typically causes members the most concern, for it forces a move past denial. In one exercise used during this step, members are asked to list their resentments and then move from the faults of other people to an acknowledgment of their own faults and fears. In others words, it forces a realization that our resentments toward others are related to our own character defects. But this step should be a "moral inventory," both of strengths and defects. On July 21, 1965, Bill W. wrote to Don R.:

Under Step Four, I think you will find it suggested that one take a positive inventory, as well as an inventory of defects—I know that somewhere in the A.A. literature this is made clear. . . . I can say that few of us take enough inventory of our defects. Yet still others are so filled with guilt and inferiority that they are forever doing this in great exaggeration. This is the reason why we suggest taking a positive inventory of assets, so that people can get in real perspective about themselves.

Some members claim that those who have completed—really completed—a fourth step never relapse. Whether or not this is true, most members describe the process of these middle steps as a life-changing experience. Some experience a sense of change at the fifth step, as did Dick M. Note here, as with the previous quotation from his talk, the shifts in speakers, the incorporation of "others' words," and the re-accentuation of those words:

And I never will forget when I got into the Fourth and Fifth Step, that really turned my life around because I was making me a list. Now this sometimes gets difficult because you got to keep it hid, especially around my house. You know, you got to move it every thirty minutes. When I got all my list made, I called my fellow preacher and I said, "I need to come by and talk to you." He said, "What do you want to talk about?" And you know what this preacher was doing, when we were meeting in that old upstairs, we had a little room in the back. While we were holding our AA meeting, he was slipping up those stairs in back, getting in that little room in the back, and he was listening to what is going on. And he asked me, "What, you want to talk?" And I said, "Yea." And he said, "Do you want to take a Fifth Step?" And I didn't know he was anywhere in the world what I was goin' to do. And I said, "Yea." He said, "Come on down here." And I went down there. And I carried that list that I had and laid it on his desk. And he said, "Are you ready?" And I sat down and started talking. I let him have it. I guess I talked to him about an hour and a half. So when I got through, I stood up. And he said, "Are you through?" And I said, "Yea." And I was waiting for him to say, "Well, God's goin' to forgive you for this." Or, "You oughta not done that." I was waitin' to see what he was goin' say. He didn't say a word. He said, "You want this piece of paper?" I said, "Na." He tore it up. Threw it in the trash can. Now, then something come over me. I started walkin' and I was floatin'. When I left his office to my truck, I was walkin' on air. And I felt a sense of freedom that I never felt before in my life. (AA Talk)

Others have a similar experience once they complete the ninth step (when one makes direct amends), but something like this "sense of freedom", which many feel to be the "spiritual awakening" mentioned in the twelfth step, typically occurs as a result of working these middle steps. Certainly, this process contributes to the voice heard in the talks of old-timers. For speakers who have told their stories repeatedly and worked the steps thoroughly, the voice is confident and soothing, even as it moves through a range of emotions. It is not angry, strident, defensive, or blaming. It is the voice of a person who has made peace with his or her past.

The final three steps, which relate to the "how things are now" portion of AA talks, have been described as a kind of spiritual maintenance. Members of the program work these steps, often on a daily basis, as a means of continuing their spiritual progress and staying in touch with the fellowship:

10. Continued to take personal inventory and when we were wrong promptly admitted it.
11. Sought through prayer and meditation to improve our conscious contact with God *as we understood Him,* praying only for knowledge of His will for us and the power to carry that out.
12. Having had a spiritual awakening as the result of these steps, we tried to carry this message to alcoholics, and to practice these principles in all our affairs.

At the end of the day, members can assess their behavior, think about where they were wrong, then admit it, apologize, maybe even make amends, if necessary. Every morning, members are encouraged to have a quiet time of prayer and meditation, perhaps reading from a book of daily meditation, as preparation for a day of sobriety and sanity. During this time, they reenact the first three steps as they ask for "knowledge of His will." The final step asks members to provide service to the organization, to "pass it on." Hence, their work with a newcomer is called a "twelfth step call" or "twelfth step work," which is considered crucial to maintaining one's own sobriety. On November 17, 1953, Bill W. responded to a letter from Charles H., who was concerned because his desire to drink had not dissipated. Bill wrote about how Dr. Bob had experienced the same thing:

> His cure was, primarily, to engage in frantic 12th Step work. He found this would divert him when nothing else would. In fact, his peculiar condition supplied the immense drive it took to start the first group at Akron, Ohio, and keep it going after I left in 1935. Bob also spent a great deal of time broadening and deepening his own spiritual life. At long last, the urge to drink deserted him. Though I think I can safely estimate that he was really never in any great danger, so great was his earnestness. But it was a hell of a nuisance—a great trial at times, indeed.

Even when twelfth step work fails to reach a newcomer, it saves the old-timers. And the importance of helping others filters its way into the tone and ethos of the talks. Speakers typically express gratitude for being able to call their sponsors or friends in the program at any hour.

While most members of AA work the steps seriously, moving through them continuously or repeatedly, it should be emphasized that they are the *suggested* path. When Al wrote Bill W. to say that members of his group in Jackson, Michigan, were getting sober without working the steps, Bill replied on May 22, 1942:

> Please do not let anyone think that we are discouraging the idea of experiment with new presentations or methods. I am sure any local group ought to do just as it wishes with such matters. I think that we ought to be utter pragmatists—whatever works must be the right thing for us. . . . On the other hand, it would seem only right that they recognize the fact that most A.A.s are using the spiritual side of the program and declare it to be absolutely essential in nearly every case. Hundreds, if not thousands, have approached A.A. with the idea that we have a fine program psychologically; that it would still work better however if we left out the religion. In almost every case, it has been suggested that they try in their own way and so they have, only to report, in most incidences, that they haven't had much luck. These are the facts—the simple arithmetic of the situation.

Contrary to critics of the program, AA does not force the steps on members and acknowledges that some sober up without them. AA does feel, however, that working the steps is the best approach to maintaining sobriety.

6

The Twelve Traditions: Bringing a Little Order to Chaos

> Spengler imagined the culture of an epoch as a closed circle.
> But the unity of a particular culture is an *open* unity.
> —M. M. Bakhtin, "Response to a Question from
> *Novy Mir* Editorial Staff"

The culture of AA varies widely from group to group, because the organization is actually many discrete units held together by the Twelve Traditions.[1] In other words, we find in the culture of AA a structure (or unity) that is open rather than closed. The Twelve Traditions, which provide much of the structure and unity, are not really a constitution, a blueprint sketched out and then followed; rather, they are an attempt to describe a set of values that developed historically. When Bill W. wrote about them in *Twelve Steps and Twelve Traditions,* he explained them as historical lessons. We tried it other ways, he said, but this is what we found to work. A discussion of the traditions, thus, can suggest a great deal about the culture of AA and how it developed, as is the case in this chapter. The discussion here should not be regarded as anything like an "official" interpretation; one does not exist anyway. Newcomers are encouraged to embrace the traditions (they are often read at the beginning of meetings), and old-timers often evoke them to settle disputes or inform group decisions. They are not, however, enforced as law.

Tradition One. Our common welfare should come first; personal recovery depends upon A.A. unity.[2] Paradoxically, AA emphasizes the importance of group unity not by enforcing conformance to rules or laws but by allowing people to be as they are, to the point that critics see "liberty verging on license." Bill W. writes:

> We believe there isn't a fellowship on earth which lavishes more
> devoted care upon its individual members; surely there is none which

> more jealously guards the individual's right to think, talk, and act as
> he wishes. No A.A. can compel another to do anything; nobody can
> be punished or expelled. (*Twelve Steps and Twelve Traditions* 129)

Because there is not a hierarchy or an uncontested dogma, individuals
are allowed to speak as they think. The members trust that their group
conscience, which relies on open discussion, will guide the group in the
best direction.

Group unity is also important in dealing with failures. Members of AA
are often faced with newcomers who suffer periodic relapses or are not
ready to devote themselves to the program. If they became focused on
these failures, they might lose hope. Their focus has to be on the health
of the group. One sometimes hears comments like "We have to let that
one go." Or "He is not ready yet." Ted H. commented: "I don't work
with people that will not . . . The Book says, the directions, there's the
person that cannot or will not accept this program. Move on. Get on with
somebody else and help them" (AA Talk). To outsiders this might seem
harsh. We are more used to organizations that make heroic efforts to save
every individual. In AA, there is more a sense that you can only help alcoholics become sober when they are ready to be helped. This principle
was evident by the time that Bill W. and Dr. Bob found Bill D., their first
successful convert. Kurtz writes:

> Wilson and Smith . . . stressed that they *had to* give their "program"
> to someone else if they were to stay sober, so was Bill D. really cer-
> tain that he wanted it? Because if he did not, he was doing worse
> than wasting their time, he was endangering their sobriety. So they
> had to know, because if he did not want it, they were not going to
> stay and nag at him. For their own sakes, they would have to "be
> going and looking for someone else." (38–39)

One final point. In a chapter entitled "The Ecology of the Bacchae,"
O'Reilly writes of the belief in alcohol's power to efface individual differences and create the sense, whether real or not, of a unity with others
(*Sobering Tales* 19–76). Much of the culture of AA provides a supple-
ment for the lost effects of drinking. Where alcoholics once believed that
they could only belong to a group and develop friendships with alcohol,
they find in AA a group identity and friendships while sober. In his analysis of alcoholism, Gregory Bateson argues that the alcoholic subjectively
experiences being sober as an "error" (i.e., as being abnormal); the alcoholic is drawn to the experience of intoxication because it seems "right"
(or normal). For AA to work, it must thus provide some way of allowing alcoholics to experience sobriety as normal. It does this (I am suggesting here and will develop in detail later) by replacing what were once

viewed as the positive outcomes of drinking with a spiritual contact with a higher power and an intense fellowship within meetings. One might argue that even the discourse of AA has much in common with the discourse of the barroom.

Tradition Two. For our group purpose there is but one ultimate authority—a loving God as He may express Himself in our group conscience. Our leaders are but trusted servants; they do not govern. When explaining this tradition, Bill W. uses the hypothetical example of two members who start a new group and, given the nature of the human ego, soon begin to feel it is *their* group, at least until they are deposed by the group conscience. In what reads like a parable, Bill W. writes of the reactions of the two founding members:

> Ultimately, they divide into two classes known in A.A. slang as "elder statesman" and "bleeding deacons." The elder statesman is the one who sees the wisdom of the group's decision, who holds no resentment over his reduced status, whose judgment, fortified by considerable experience, is sound, and who is willing to sit quietly on the sidelines patiently awaiting developments. The bleeding deacon is one who is just as surely convinced that the group cannot get along without him, who constantly connives for reelection to office, and who continues to be consumed with self-pity. A few hemorrhage so badly that—drained of all A.A. spirit and principle—they get drunk. At times the A.A. landscape seems to be littered with bleeding forms. Nearly every oldtimer in our society has gone through this process to some degree. (*Twelve Steps and Twelve Traditions* 135)

Bill W. goes on to recount how he, cofounder of AA, enthusiastically proposed a new idea to *his* group (which met at *his* house). The group told Bill it was a bad idea. He accepted the group's decision. Later, he admitted they were right.

From Bill W.'s description of the function of "group conscience" in the *Twelve Steps and Twelve Traditions,* outsiders might start to feel, with a waxing cynicism, that AA is being presented as an organization of a great bunch of people who just naturally get along. Actually, the history of AA is filled with acrimonious squabbles. As but one example, after an AA dinner in Cleveland in 1941, Bill W. and Dr. Bob were taken to a hotel room and accused of using the organization in order to prosper financially from the publication of *Alcoholics Anonymous.* Perhaps because he expected the issue to be raised at some point, Bill had a certified audit of the books with him. Dr. Bob had received no royalties; his income came from his medical practice, which he was then attempting to rebuild, and a $30 a week stipend from the Rockefeller Foundation. Bill, who devoted all of his time to building the organization, drew $25 a week from book sales; he also received a $30 a week Rockefeller stipend (*'Pass It On'* 255–57).

Bill W. felt that differences of opinion were healthy, as long as one does not become self-righteous. In a January 3, 1951, letter to Lois K., he wrote:

> Out at Detroit, Chuck feels that he has to save A.A. from George. At New York, some of my best friends seem deeply convinced that A.A. has to be saved from me, no holds barred. Differences of opinion ought to be healthy. But when anger and spleen take on the garb of noble purpose, no constructive difference of opinion is possible. Everybody gets hurt, nothing is settled. Surely enough, it is the thoroughly well-meaning people who are so often prone to this phoney virtue. I have often victimized myself and others with it. I noted that a number of us old-timers exhibit the same tendency. But must we always learn the hard way?

Throughout his correspondence, Bill W. encourages members to allow the petty squabbles to run their course. On February 1, 1950, for example, he wrote to Clarence D.: "A.A. has a marvelous capacity for self-adjustment. The worst that can happen will come in the form of a few headaches." Flynn observed far more infighting at central-office and intergroup meetings, where the focus is on coordinating local and regional activities, than at group meetings, where the focus in on maintaining sobriety (66), which is consistent with my observations. Indeed, it could be argued that the central office and intergroup meetings provide a space to "vent the spleen" and, as a result, serve the function of keeping group meetings virtually free of contentious debate.

Tradition Three. The only requirement for A.A. membership is a desire to stop drinking. Basically, this tradition states that anyone who wants to attend meetings (this is the provisional gage of a desire to stop drinking) can be a member. There are no membership applications or committees to evaluate who should be let in or kept out. There are no initiation rituals. One becomes a member by attending meetings and saying, "I am a member." Members do not even have to stay sober. Some, I have observed, come to meetings drunk. These people in the midst of a relapse are typically remorseful, weeping through most of the meeting. They are treated with respect and usually surrounded by members at the end of the meeting who hand over phone numbers. "It is just not a big deal," one member told me.

Again, this is the norm. Exceptions do occur. For example, alcoholics (especially old-timers) sometimes become upset when drug addicts attend AA meetings (rather than Narcotics Anonymous meetings). Thus, many alcoholics who are also drug addicts simply describe themselves as alcoholics at AA meetings.

Tradition Four. Each group should be autonomous except in matters affecting other groups or A.A. as a whole. As each individual is left to find his or her way, each group is left to determine its own structure and rituals. Contrary to the management theory of the time, AA believed that group unity came from openness rather than rules. Bill W. writes:

> When A.A.'s Traditions were first published, in 1946, we had become sure that an A.A. group could stand almost any amount of battering. We saw that the group, exactly like the individual, must eventually conform to whatever tested principles would guarantee survival. We had discovered that there was perfect safety in the process of trial and error. (*Twelve Steps and Twelve Traditions* 146)

Bill goes on to tell of one group that adopted sixty-one rules and regulations. When a "chill chokedamp of fear and frustration fell over the group," they wrote rule sixty-two: "Don't take yourself too damn seriously."

Essentially, what this tradition means is that each group is free to develop its own culture; thus, any given town or city will develop a diversity of groups. There are women's groups and men's groups, smoking groups and nonsmoking groups, lunch groups and breakfast groups, biker groups and banker groups. Individuals can thus find a group that fits their needs. As a result of this diversity, some of the gossip that occurs outside of meetings might be regarded as criticism of groups rather than individuals. One might hear a member say, "I don't feel comfortable in that meeting." Or "That's not a healthy group."

One can speak of general AA traditions as well as variations that occur at the national, regional, local, and group levels. For example, a long-established group in Texas elects a president who then administers the business of the group; most members would consider such action a violation of the ninth tradition (discussed later in this chapter). For this reason, Maxwell warns that outsiders might be "mislead by A.A. group phenomena which we may observe in certain local groups or hear from certain individual members, unless we can also become aware of the fellowship-wide patterns and trends" ("Alcoholics Anonymous" 298).

Tradition Five. Each group has but one primary purpose—to carry its message to the alcoholic who still suffers. Before this expression of a need for group unity come several traditions that basically say, "Do what you like." So how is unity expressed and achieved? It is expressed and achieved through unity of purpose. The group exists solely to help its members remain sober—to carry the message. This tradition carries special force because of the material events that surround it. When someone is telling his or her story, one often hears, "AA saved my life." This is not a hyperbole. The members of AA periodically see friends relapse and die. Speakers often comment on the loss of close friends to the "disease." It is extremely difficult to convey the power of such statements—and the effect that they have on promoting group unity—to the outsider.

While I was attending open AA meetings, I frequently heard members speak of the death of friends, both practicing alcoholics outside the program and struggling members inside the program. Often, members see a death coming, sometimes as long as a year in advance. Outside of a meeting, they might say, "He may not make it." Or they might challenge the member directly during a meeting. After the death, the lost friend remains a part of the group's discussions. While a particular group may not lose one of its members frequently, examples of the deadly consequences of alcoholism are frequently discussed and observed.

In his analysis of alcoholic thinking, Bateson emphasizes the body and the environment. He comments on the AA "test" for those who are convinced that they are not alcoholics, that they go to the "nearest barroom and try some controlled drinking." If the person is an alcoholic, then he or she will fail. Bateson says: "We might compare the test . . . to commanding a driver to brake suddenly when traveling on a slippery road: he will discover fast that his control is limited" (330). In other words, the discourse of AA is grounded in a material reality that serves as a rather powerful authority.

Tradition Six. An A.A. group ought never endorse, finance, or lend the A.A. name to any related facility or outside enterprise, lest problems of money, property, and prestige divert us from our primary purpose. Bill W. believed that alcoholics are people with big ideas. Once early members of AA discovered what they felt was the answer to the problem of alcoholism, they began to think about building hospitals, making money, and even changing the world. They had to learn quickly that the values of their greater society (making money, accumulating property, and achieving fame) or the endorsement of political causes (which, they believed, damaged the Washingtonians) would disrupt the unity and purpose of AA.

And so one finds in any given group a wide range of values and beliefs without arguments about who is right. Catholics, Baptists, Jews, and Muslims talk about God or their higher power. Republicans, Democrats, and Libertarians talk about their struggles with sobriety, but they do not talk about politics. Newcomers, who have not yet learned the traditions, might make political comments, but it is the custom of old-timers to let them pass without response. In a June 24, 1949, letter to Frank L., Bill W. wrote: "None of us have the slightest desire, or even tries to interfere with another member's religion or political beliefs or activities. The reason is simple: as a fellowship we do not wish to commit suicide."

Tradition Seven. Every A.A. group ought to be fully self-supporting, declining outside contributions. When explaining this tradition, Bill W. writes: "One A.A. group was given five thousand dollars to do with what it would. The hassle over that chunk of money played havoc for years" (*Twelve Steps and Twelve Traditions* 161). Again, we see a distrust of money that sets this organization apart from other kinds of organizations, even many spiritual institutions. At AA meetings, the basket is passed;

most toss in a dollar. If someone declines to contribute (maybe they don't have change, or maybe they cannot afford it), nothing is ever said. Another example of how AA tends to break class divisions is shown in a June 9, 1942, letter to Larry J. Bill W. wrote:

> We are all so skeptical of setting up groups for special classes of people. While the sooner that people of wealth or special position realize they have a fatal and progressive disease which may require them to get rid of some of their inhibitions, the better. In A.A. groups elsewhere, people of like tastes naturally see more of each other, yet there is in these groups a pretty general feeling that every alcoholic who wishes to get well is "one of the right people" regardless of his social status.

People who are unemployed or earning minimum wage throw in a dollar, if they can afford it; people who are worth millions throw in a dollar.

Tradition Eight. Alcoholics Anonymous should remain forever nonprofessional, but our service centers may employ special workers. This tradition discourages hiring a professional to do "twelfth step calls," run meetings, plan conventions, and so on, because the "money motive compromises him and everything he says and does" (*Twelve Steps and Twelve Traditions* 166). People might be hired to answer the phones and such, but the real work is done by members. In most larger cities, the organization has an intergroup (comprised of volunteers) that coordinates activities, publishes a newsletter, sells books, and perhaps organizes conventions. They may have an office, but it is usually staffed by volunteers as well.

Tradition Nine. A.A., as such, ought never be organized; but we may create service boards or committees directly responsible to those they serve. Bill W. explains: "Though Tradition Nine at first sight seems to deal with a purely practical matter, in its actual operation it discloses a society without organization, animated only by the spirit of service—a true fellowship" (*Twelve Steps and Twelve Traditions* 175). It also means that no AA board or committee "can issue a single directive to an A.A. member and make it stick, let alone mete out any punishment" (172). AA certainly has its share of conflicts. But when disputes arise, they tend to run their course and then die out in a whimper. Why? They have to. No mechanism exists to resolve conflict, so no means exists for the escalation of conflict. Thus, members work out their disputes among themselves without pulling the "organization" into it. Some people might stay angry, stop attending meetings, or get drunk, but disputes between individuals remain between individuals. Members might report a controversy to a regional or national office, but they will only hear, "We can't do anything about it." Frequently, disputes are resolved by forming a new group, which is easily accomplished. As an early member said, "All you need to form a new group in A.A. is a resentment and a coffeepot" (*Dr. Bob* 166).

Ted H., when telling his story, offered the following advice for dealing with controversies within the organization:

> When you're caught in turmoil in your district or your area or your group, or, you know, with these people over there, or how they're doing it, answer every question you have about that with one question to yourself, "What does that have to do with me working with the next guy who comes through the door?" Not a damned thing. (AA Talk)

Indeed, this is how most of the members of AA deal with organizational squabbles: They realize that helping other alcoholics, which is the sole purpose of AA, happens as "one drunk talks to another." They focus on this service and let disagreements run their course.

Tradition Ten. Alcoholics Anonymous has no opinion on outside issues; hence the A.A. name ought never be drawn into public controversy. With this tradition, AA hoped to avoid the controversy that, as they believed, destroyed the Washingtonians. As mentioned before, potentially disruptive comments about political or social issues are rarely made. When they are broached, usually by a newcomer, they pass without comment. Indeed, it is typical within meetings that all comments pass without comment. A newcomer might say, "My husband is a worthless son of a bitch." Those who speak later do not say, "You shouldn't talk like that." But someone might say something like this: "I have learned in this program that I need to look to my own part in any problem. Rather than judge others, I try to own up to my own defects of character." When advice is offered, it is through personal experience—not "you should do this" but "this is how I handled a similar situation." In general, members share their own experience (it is an "I" discourse rather than a "you" discourse) while attempting to avoid judging others or attempting to change them.

Tradition Eleven. Our public relations policy is based on attraction rather than promotion; we need always maintain personal anonymity at the level of press, radio, and films. The public relations policy of "attraction" means that AA lets itself be judged by the "works" of its members, and it lets others speak in its behalf. The organization does not employ press agents, and it does not fund an advertising campaign. New members are often brought to the program by mass media stories written by outsiders, but usually it is because a friend approaches a friend and says: "I'm a member of AA. If you ever want some help, I will be glad to take you to a meeting." The practicing alcoholic sees what the AA member has and wants it. This is "attraction" rather than "promotion." The policy of anonymity with mass media prevents the association of a single personality with the program, as happened with the Oxford Group. Especially in the early years, AA was very concerned that the actions (perhaps the relapse) of a single member might compromise the perceived effectiveness of AA as a whole, but again we see the need to hold "personal ambition" in check. Individuals should not use AA to achieve fame or profit from their membership.

Tradition Twelve. Anonymity is the spiritual foundation of all our traditions, ever reminding us to place principles before personalities. Most outsiders assume that the sole function of AA's policy of anonymity is to protect individuals from experiencing public shame, but this is rarely an issue for people who have been in the program more than a few months. Anonymity is also seen as a way of downplaying the ill effects of inflated personæ and thus promoting group harmony.

Anonymity certainly checks the dangers of pride and greed, but it also creates new ways of knowing others. Since members tend to know each other by first name only, they may refer to others by adding description ("Joan the redhead") or some personal quality ("Bob the banker" or "the quiet John"). What is difficult to describe is how this pushes one past perfunctory ways of getting to know others; referring to someone by full name does not force a consciousness of an individual's profession, appearance, or personal qualities. What anonymity means is that within AA, one comes to know others in a different way than one comes to know people outside the program. Through anonymity (the diminished importance of names within AA), one overcomes anonymity (the hiding behind names outside the program).

Anonymity can, on occasions, be broken. If a member can help someone else by declaring an affiliation with AA, then it is appropriate to do so. Also, as one's recovery progresses, after one feels comfortable with a new identity within AA, he or she might tell others outside the program—but not the media—to "lose his fear of the alcoholic stigma" (*Twelve Steps and Twelve Traditions* 186). The anonymity is AA's "spiritual foundation" because it promotes a sense of trust, but also because it promotes a sense of sacrifice and service: "Because A.A.'s Twelve Traditions repeatedly ask us to give up personal desires for the common good, we realize that the sacrificial spirit—well symbolized by anonymity—is the foundation of them all" (184).

Part Two

Storytelling

7

The Author and the Hero: Uncertainty, Freedom, and Rigorous Honesty

> The vast majority of novels (and subcategories of novels) know only the image of the *ready-made* hero.
> —M. M. Bakhtin, "The *Bildungsroman*"

> Rarely have we seen a person fail who has thoroughly followed our path. Those who do not recover are people who cannot or will not completely give themselves to this simple program, usually men and women who are constitutionally incapable of being honest with themselves. There are such unfortunates. They are not at fault; they seem to have been born that way. They are naturally incapable of grasping and developing a manner of living which demands rigorous honesty.
> —*Alcoholics Anonymous*

L illian Roth—movie star, alcoholic, member of AA—begins *I'll Cry Tomorrow,* the first of her autobiographies, without seeming to know *how* to begin:

> I have thought of many ways to start my story. I could begin it at a moment of triumph, when as a Hollywood star my escorts to a world premiere were Gary Cooper and Maurice Chevalier, when three of my pictures were running simultaneously on Broadway, and I earned $3,500 for an afternoon's work. This would be a glamorous beginning.
>
> I could begin it at an awful moment, when I stood before an open window, behind me years of alcoholic horror and degradation, about to leap to the pavement eleven stories below. That would be a melodramatic beginning.
>
> Or I could begin it at the age of thirty-four, when as an ex-inmate of a mental institution, I was released to start my life over again.

> But that might be a puzzling beginning, and difficult for some to understand.
>
> Perhaps, as my husband Burt suggests, the way to tell it is the way it happened, allowing it to unfold in the order dictated by whatever mysterious forces mold us into the persons we become. "That's the only way it will make sense," he cautioned me. "Tell it as it happened."
>
> This is how it happened, then. (13)

She begins in the way that stories are typically told at AA meetings. This moment of self-consciousness about her narrative, the sense that she does not know how to begin or proceed, rambling as if giving voice to private thoughts and then suddenly being aware that she is actually speaking— in this case writing—to others, occasionally apologizing for the lack of form, but mostly lost in the telling.

Then her husband says, "Tell it as it happened." And Roth does. She moves into traditional autobiography (actually coauthored with Mike Connolly and Gerold Frank). It is a well-written narrative, with a plot, a moral, a sense of completeness, even though she is writing about the life that she is still living. She is, throughout, writing *for* (rather than *before*) an audience, as is clear even in the preface, even before the reader encounters her self-conscious beginning. In "A Note to the Reader," it is clear that she has a rhetorical purpose:

> I recall the mingled hope and fear I felt not so long ago when my story was sketched on Ralph Edward's "This Is Your Life" program. I was told a television audience of 40,000,000 people would see me as I came on the stage.
>
> I thought then, almost desperately, *"What will they think of me? Will they remember that I was once famous and then infamous? That I was a drunk for so many years? Will they think that I am flaunting my past or making a bid for sympathy? . . ."*
>
> Some of these emotions are mine now. Why *am* I writing this book? The reasons are mixed. For one thing, I believe the very writing will help clarify myself in relation to the world about me. I think it will help reestablish my integrity in my own eyes, and I hope it will help reestablish my integrity and my dignity in the eyes of those who knew me when I had neither. (9)

If Roth were speaking before an AA meeting, she would not be telling her story in this way for this purpose. Similar to the storytelling of the Washingtonians, her autobiography is a narrative by an alcoholic written for an audience that is primarily nonalcoholic. She feels a need to justify herself, explain her actions, seek forgiveness, and restore her reputation and dignity. When speaking to other alcoholics within the setting of an AA meeting, this is all simply irrelevant.

Even more importantly, Roth writes as if her life were finished, as if she could give the reader a complete account, as if she could "clarify" herself "in relation to the world around" her. But she could not. After Roth finished *I'll Cry Tomorrow,* her life continued. So she wrote another autobiography, *Beyond My Worth.* In the new book, written without coauthors, she tells of her struggles to build a career as a nightclub singer and her search for a home, but she also tells of how people in crisis seek her out. Why? Because they have read *I'll Cry Tomorrow* and Roth is, it seems to them, a person who has solved all of her problems and so can help them to solve theirs. Roth writes in her new book:

> We are not always what we seem to be to others. The people who came to me with their troubles no doubt believed me to be a strong person. Yet, at the time I was, and I still am to a degree filled with the same emotional conflicts that most of us harbor in varying quantities. We all have our hopes, desires, dreams, and fears. Yet so much good was happening to me that my guilt was heavy when I did not try in some measure to lighten their burden. In a way this was difficult because I still had a rough road to travel and if I did not make it right to the very end, I would not be much good to myself or anyone else. Not everything is as it looks, either. In the eyes of my unseen friends, I had made it. Only I knew what a darn tough battle was in store for me. (43)

In *Beyond My Worth,* Roth seems to want to revive the hero of *I'll Cry Tomorrow,* show that this "character" continues to struggle with life and self, and yet she finishes the "character" off again in the last chapter. The hero and her husband, who loves her "beyond her worth," have moved into her first home; she has also made the decision to return to acting, even if it means giving up a lucrative career as a singer. She seems once again to have made it. And there it ends.

Roth's autobiographies are not AA stories. While they tell the story of an alcoholic, they also attempt to reach a fullness and finality that readers of autobiography expect. In autobiography, according to Bakhtin, the author attempts to give a full account of "the basic and typical aspects of any life course" ("The *Bildungsroman*" 17). The hero's development "is the result of the entire totality of changing life circumstances and events, activity and work" (22). Although AA stories have autobiographical moments, they are much more and much less. They lack the completeness of autobiography or of a full narrative, so the hero remains unfinished, never fully captured or defined. Bakhtin would say that the hero is not consummated.

In "Author and Hero in Aesthetic Activity," Bakhtin begins with an epistemic problem (how is it that we can know others, or that others can know us?) that he eventually approaches from the perspective of aesthetics (how do we, as readers, perceive the relationship between the author and the central character of a text, whom Bakhtin calls the "hero"?). Bakhtin sets up the epistemic problem in this way: I know myself only as an interior; I know others as an exterior. In other words, I can know my own consciousness—my thoughts, sensations, emotions—but I can never know how others *sense* me. If I look in a mirror, touch my face, or listen to the sound of my voice, I can never completely objectify myself. Conversely, others remain objects for me. I can see their bodies, hear their voices, touch their skin, but I can never truly enter their thoughts. Given this basic separation of self and other, Bakhtin goes on to ask, what happens when an author creates a character, a hero, in a text? We do not have, Bakhtin argues, the kind of simple correspondence that is often found in naïve biographical criticism: the belief that the author *is* the hero. Rather, we have in the relationship between author and hero the same kind of complex dynamics entailed in the relationship between self and other. One of the most important distinctions that Bakhtin makes between author and hero is that the author is unconsummated (still working through the unfolding events of a life in progress), while the hero in most texts is consummated (even as we begin the first page of a novel, even though we, as readers, may not know how the story will end, the hero's life has already been written). In Bakhtin's words:

> If I am consummated and my life is consummated, I am no longer capable of living and acting. For in order to live and act, I need to be unconsummated, I need to be open to myself—at least in all the essential moments constituting my life; I have to be, for myself, someone who is axiologically yet-to-be, someone who does not coincide with his already existing makeup. (13)

Bakhtin does not set up a simple dichotomy here. He begins with a basic proposition: The author is unconsummated (living an unfinished life); the hero is consummated (a character who is fated, in a sense, to act the events of a completed narrative). But, for Bakhtin, this basic distinction is never pure.[1] The heroes in some genres are more consummated than those in others. Even in a single text, with a plot that moves through all of the conventions of a particular genre, when the hero seems to be consummated by both the author and the tradition in which the author works, there are moments when the interior of the author seems to penetrate the exterior of the hero, or the interior of the hero seems to penetrate the author, as the author fixes his or her identity in the creation of a hero and then becomes something else or remains something more.[2] There are also moments when the life of the reader crosses the lives of the author and hero. Bakhtin refers to these moments of shared values as being axiological, and they form, for him, the basis of aesthetic and ultimately ethical experience.[3]

When Roth wrote *I'll Cry Tomorrow* to explain herself and save her reputation, she created a hero. The hero, consummated and finished, allowed her to make sense of her yet unfinished life as situated in a moral tableaux. Because readers come to know the happy ending of her conquering alcoholism, they can forgive her. And if Roth can write an ending to her life, she can feel that she is past her drinking days. This is why we find so much pleasure in reading about finished lives: They have a sense of certainty that we, as living and changing human beings, crave. But Roth soon found that the hero she had created in *I'll Cry Tomorrow* was not who she had become.

As we move further into an analysis of AA stories, we will see that they are not print autobiographies, like *I'll Cry Tomorrow* or *Beyond My Worth*. They do not achieve a fullness of plot, and the heroes are not fully consummated. The stories have a certain form in that the speakers tell how they used to be, how they became involved with AA, and how they are now, but we hear only fragments of a life that trail off without a clear ending. The speaker, in effect, says, "I see my life going in a positive direction, but things could change quickly." They are unfinished tales about learning to live with uncertainty.

It is this kind of openness and freedom that Bakhtin found so compelling about the works of Dostoevsky. Morson writes:

> Bakhtin dwells on Dostoevsky's most surprising self-characterization. "I am not a psychologist." If Dostoevsky is not a psychologist, we may ask, then who is? As Bakhtin understands this gnomic statement, Dostoevsky meant to reject the *wrong sort* of psychology, which treats people as the "ready-made" product of pregiven psychic drives. For all their similarity in some respects, Freud and Dostoevsky part company on this fundamental issue. For Dostoevsky, to understand people is to comprehend not their predetermination but their freedom. ("Prosaic Bakhtin" 37)

One of the ways that Dostoevsky allows characters freedom is in his use of plot. Morson and Emerson write that Dostoevsky "avoids using a character's predetermined destiny as a way of 'ambushing' and 'finalizing' him. Instead, plot becomes a way of setting optimally favorable situations for intense dialogues with unforeseen outcomes" (247).

What Bakhtin ultimately values in Dostoevsky is freedom: a way of telling a life story that does not predict a certain outcome. Bakhtin realized that fiction or autobiography, as genres that develop historically into norms, exerting expectations upon the author, could shape the creation of a hero in a way that would limit the author's ability to come to knowledge of the self through writing (a clean narrative can hide as well as reveal) and then change (a clean narrative can predict a certain ending). Of course, the author's creation of any hero in any genre could potentially become the means of achieving self-knowledge, but some genres are more rigid than others. As I will argue in later chapters, the genre of AA stories allows for a high degree of openness, but we need also to realize that the culture of AA, the context in which AA stories are told, provides a social support for speakers as they move toward a more honest view of themselves, which lays the foundation for a shift in identity. The movement toward greater honesty is particularly crucial for alcoholics.

By the time that alcoholics bottom out, they have learned to tell outlandish lies convincingly; perhaps they have lied to themselves for so long that their lies seem as believable as the truths that they work so hard to deny. Yet, telling lies to cover the lies and trying to keep track of what was said to whom eventually takes it toll. As Dick M. says: "I wanta tell you it's a job to stay drunk. It's a twenty-four hour job. But it's not that hard to stay sober" (AA Talk). At some point most alcoholics become so worn down that their lies fall apart. They look in the mirror with a little more honesty. And it seems that some degree of reality, some honesty about self, must occur before an alcoholic can even conceive of a need to stop drinking.

But is it possible to achieve "rigorous honesty," without which the newcomer to AA will fail? Can we really be honest with others in a post-Freudian age? More importantly, can we learn to be honest with ourselves? It seems that our modern consciousness speaks always in the presence of others, speaking not what we want or need to say, but speaking in a way that anticipates a negative response, even when others are not bodily present, even when we think we are speaking in our own minds, apparently in isolation. It is this speaking as if we are already in dialogue with others, expecting their criticism, not knowing if even our confessions are truthful, that Bakhtin calls the sideward glance. It is speaking and looking out of the corner of one's eye at the same time, straining to see how someone else will react to our words while we pretend not to care, while we convince ourselves that *they* are not influencing how *we* speak. It is also, although Bakhtin did not conceive of it in this way, an accurate description of alcoholic thinking, a dishonest way of being with others that alcoholics must learn to move past—if they are to tell their stories with honesty and change.

When Bakhtin discusses the sideward glance, he uses examples from Dostoevsky's "Notes from the Underground." The narrator of this short novel is attempting to confess, be honest to others, and account for his forty years of life. He denies all concern for what his audience thinks, but he constantly anticipates how "they"—some vague group of gentlemen—will react. The following is a fairly typical passage:

> Here one could not blame even the laws of nature, though the laws of nature have, in fact, always and more than anything else caused me infinite worry and trouble all through my life. It is disgusting to call to mind all this, and as a matter of fact it was a disgusting busi-

ness even then. For after a minute or so I used to realize bitterly that it was all a lie, a horrible lie, a hypocritical lie, I mean, all those repentances, all those emotional outbursts, all those promises to turn over a new leaf. And if you ask why I tormented myself like that, the answer is because I was awfully bored sitting about and doing nothing, and that is why I started on that sort of song and dance. I assure you it is true. You'd better start watching yourselves more closely, gentlemen, and you will understand that it is so. I used to invent my own adventures, I used to devise my own life for myself, so as to be able to carry on somehow. How many times, for instance, used I to take offence without rhyme or reason, deliberately; and of course I realised very well that I had taken offence at nothing, that the whole thing was just a piece of play-acting, but in the end I would work myself up into such a state that I would be offended in good earnest. All my life I felt drawn to play such tricks, so that in the end I simply lost control of myself. (275–76)

What happens, he asks the gentlemen, if you allow yourself to be "carried away by your emotions blindly"? He answers, "[Y]ou will begin despising yourself for having knowingly duped yourself."

The sideward glance describes how the voices of others enter our consciousness—indeed, are the very nature of our consciousness. We can see it when we watch conversations around us. Two people are sitting face to face as one says: "And then he said, 'I don't want to go to your parents' house.' And I said, 'Why not? Aren't they good enough for you?' And he just looked at me. It made me so mad. I just wanted to hit him. So he said . . ." As some conversation with another person is internalized, we begin to develop personalities within our heads that tell us what to think and feel.

In Bakhtin's theory, all discourse contains multiple voices, but he distinguishes between monoglossia (the monologic, in which a single voice emerges as dominant) and polyglossia (the dialogic, in which other voices are not marginalized). In Palmer's interpretation, these terms should be viewed within a continuum that describes how power is related to the use of language:

> [I]f there are no languages that exist outside of or before the advent of power (even if such power simply manifests itself as the desire among speakers to think of their different varieties as sharing something essential in common), it is certainly the case that languages differ in the extent to which their system of varieties is controlled or regulated. This means that we may retain the terms heteroglossia and monoglossia to designate the extremes of such a continuum (i.e., tolerant pluralism and repressive authoritarianism). A very useful result of this revision is the changed status it accords to monoglossia, which no longer appears as a perversion of the natural, but rather as the inevitable other of heteroglossia. Such a view, in fact, is not

far removed from what Bakhtin occasionally says of himself when he, correctly and perceptively, identifies monoglossia with the centripetal forces of language and heteroglossia with the centrifugal (this metaphor from physics nicely images the dialectic relationships between these two language modes). And yet this neutral account is often contradicted by an evaluative one in which heteroglossia is offered as the originary (and hence preferred) term. (104–5)

So even monoglossia, in forms such as the "sideward glance," "is hardly itself a unified or essential category" (105). It is not, however, dialogic in that it is not "pluralistic," a "cooperative and mutually respectful co-presence of languages," a "plurality of unmixed voices" (107, 113).

Speakers at AA meetings often comment on the voices in their heads (the internalized others that constitute the sideward glance) and the need to sort them out, the need to find some clarity and sanity amid the buzz of their mental crowd. Bill W. referred to this buzz of voices as a "dry drunk," and it is often referred to as lapsing back into alcoholic thinking. It may even take on a spatial sense: It is the kind of thinking that occurs "out there," outside of the program. Dr. Paul O. says:

> My head is full of personalities. And they talk, and they talk, and they talk. That's all they do. They just talk. They never do my work. They just talk, and they talk. Day or night, they talk. Even at night they talk. Sometimes, they just ruin my night. And sometimes, I wake up and my day is ruined and it hasn't even started yet. . . . My life isn't determined by what happens. The quality of my life is determined by what they think happens and who I listen to. The one up there, no matter what happens, he says, "Boy, are you getting screwed. Ya, you're really getting it now." If I listen to him, my day is ruined. (AA Talk)

Alcoholic thinking is often talked about and, as Dr. Paul does above, parodied by being juxtaposed against the more "sane" discourse of AA, which members feel is a calmer and more spiritual way of thinking. Later in his story, Dr. Paul speaks of how he moves past the voices in his head when he practices prayer or meditation or when he helps another alcoholic. As discussed earlier, when members of AA are making twelfth step calls, they are in the persona of the program and, so, outside of themselves and their own struggles.

The movement beyond the sideward glance is found first with one's higher power, but then it enlarges to include one's sponsor, fellow alcoholics, and even people outside the program. Kurtz explains how the "telling of personal experience" is a move toward honesty, a move past denial to acceptance of being an alcoholic:

> The sober alcoholic told his own story out of the conviction that such honesty was required only by and necessary only to his own sobri-

ety. This example was evidence of the A.A. understanding that honesty was necessary to *get* sobriety. Rather than any direct attack upon the mechanisms of denial or the evidence of self-centeredness, the carrier of the program of Alcoholics Anonymous demonstrated literally and vividly the essential necessity of honesty to his own sobriety. This honesty basic to identification concerned precisely the speaker's weakness and vulnerability: he bared his internal torment while drinking—in this very act being further vulnerable—*now even to this listener.* (61)

This storytelling, Kurtz remarks, is "offered without any demand for reciprocity or for anything else" (61). In Bakhtin's terms, the program moves newcomers from the "sideward glance" to the dialogic by allowing members to speak without the expectation of a direct response.

AA stories are certainly dialogic (a "plurality of unmixed voices") in the broader sense that one speaker's story is followed by another's. Each person learns not just from the telling but also from how his or her story positions itself within the context of other people's stories. The stories move from the monologic, the "sideward glance," because each person's story is told, as will be explained in subsequent chapters, to *listeners who only listen.* If they respond, it is with their bodies—with nods, tears, laughter, hugs. This constitutes a movement past the sideward glance, past speaking in anticipation of a negative response, past speaking to marginalize other voices.

Those who have been in the program for a while frequently comment on how they feel that they are able to be honest at meetings. I have heard old-timers say, "It is nice to come to a place where no one cares what I say." They do not mean that the audience does not listen. Rather, they mean they will not be criticized for saying what would be taboo in other settings. While it can certainly be argued that we can never be completely honest, as we play roles for others, even for ourselves when we are alone, even without realizing it, people nonetheless feel that they find a greater degree of honesty in AA meetings. They feel that they can make controversial comments without offending others or without being judged. They feel that they move past the sideward glance, the need to alter what they want to say because some people—some "gentlemen"—out there might criticize them. How is it that some sense of honesty is achieved? There's a simple answer: It's the entire program. It has to do with acceptance, the attempt to avoid dogma, the use of satire and humor, the special relationship between sponsor and sponsee, confidentiality, anonymity, the elimination of cross talk, and an approach to telling one's story that does not "finalize" the hero, as we will see in later chapters. The movement toward honesty, however, begins with the first confession: "I am an alcoholic."

8

I Am an Alcoholic: The First Confession

> Selfishness—self-centeredness! That, we think, is the root of
> our troubles. Driven by a hundred forms of fear, self-delusion,
> self-seeking, and self-pity, we step on the toes of our fellows
> and they retaliate. Sometimes they hurt us, seemingly with-
> out provocation, but we invariably find that at some time in
> the past we have made decisions based on self which later
> placed us in a position to be hurt.
>
> —*Alcoholics Anonymous*

> I just kept on drinking between meetings. I just kept on drink-
> ing till I was through. Until I became an alcoholic. That's what
> it was. I went to that one meeting too many, and I caught the
> disease. That's what happened to me. I wasn't an alcoholic
> when I came here.
>
> —Dr. Paul O., AA Talk

The stories told at meetings of Alcoholics Anonymous can, in part,
be more "rigorously honest" because one "drunk talks to another."
A sense of identity and acceptance begins with the first time that a newcomer says with a quivering voice, "I am an alcoholic." In time, the newcomer will be able to speak the same phrase with little emotion, even a
calm sense of pride. The semantic content of the phrase has not changed,
but, Bakhtin would argue, the intonation has. Bakhtin even says that in
some exchanges, it is intonation alone that conveys the message:

> To a certain degree, one can speak by means of intonation alone,
> making the verbally expressed part of speech relative and replace-
> able, almost indifferent. How often we use words whose meaning is
> unnecessary, or repeat the same word or phrase, just in order to have
> a material bearer for some necessary intonation. ("Toward a Meth-
> odology" 166)

It is this shift in intonation, a rather subtle change, one that outsiders might frequently overlook, that marks a transformation in identity. What precipitates the change? Bakhtin would say that it is the response it receives.

If Bill W. were to tell his story within the current oral tradition of Alcoholics Anonymous, he would begin by saying, "Hello, I'm Bill. I'm an alcoholic." Bakhtin calls this phrase an utterance, a whole unit of communication that might be as short as a grunt or as long as a book. The audience would respond by saying, "Hello, Bill." Their response is also an utterance, which forms a dialogic exchange that is surprisingly complex. O'Reilly writes:

> A great deal is accomplished in short compass . . . I will not insist that all of these things happen every time "I'm an alcoholic" is uttered; rote usage by oldtimers and experimentation by the unconvinced are among the possible exceptions to full-bodied sincerity. But there is surely a sufficiency of communicative richness here to challenge reductive synopsis. "Alcoholic"—a problematic designation in any case—becomes a multifaceted token, fusing medical, philosophical, social, and imaginative aspects of a situation whose evolution is not complete, perhaps deliberately confusing them, perhaps aspiring toward an ambiguity so dense that it generates its own independent symbolic authority. (*Sobering Tales* 155)

By offering only his first name, Bill is working out of the organization's tradition of anonymity, which facilitates honesty as it discourages "a cult of personality," an inflation of the individual's sense of importance. The salutation is quickly followed by a confession, the first of many, that establishes his authority: He is one who is entitled to speak about the subject of alcoholism. The confession also establishes a sense of community. As he says, "I am an alcoholic," he says, "I am one of you." As the audience responds, "Hello Bill," they say, "We too are alcoholics; we will accept what you have to say without judging you."

This ritual is repeated by every member, maybe several times during a single meeting, and, as Michael K. has written, its meaning changes with each utterance. It is a rhetorical act that transforms. Michael K. wrote of the first time he uttered the phrase "I am an alcoholic":

> My life was in ruins. I had the shakes. All was a blur. The academic community to which I belong seemed to disapprove of my actions. But I wasn't completely sure if they disapproved or not. I wasn't even sure which specific actions were offensive. I told people that I was a "heavy drinker." I think they believed me, and only disapproved of my actions. I felt judged. I felt angry. I drank to escape my resentment. Things became more blurry. I met a friend with whom I teach. He seemed serene. He did not judge me. He told me about A.A.—

and that he belonged to A.A. I asked him if belonging made him feel serene. I laughed. It seemed like a joke. He told me that he was an alcoholic. I denied that I was an alcoholic. He asked me if I would like to attend an A.A. meeting. I said maybe—if it would make me feel serene and make him even more serene. I asked him what was required. He said only one thing: "say that you're an alcoholic." I laughed. I drank and drank, and then everything seemed like a *dream*. I told my friend that I thought I might be an alcoholic. I attended a meeting of A.A., but I did not say that I was an alcoholic. Everybody seemed—well, not serene, but at peace with themselves and with the other people there. I got drunk. I wanted to belong—but I could not say the words. The dream deepened. I went to a second meeting, and somehow, for some reason, I said "I am an alcoholic." I am still not completely sure what my motive was for saying the words. My throat thickened. My knees buckled. Everything had been changed. *I* had been changed. I had said only four words, and I experienced a kind of immediate *transcendence*. I was no longer what I had been. (155)

Bill W. and Michael K. *were* alcoholics before they said the words; some would say they were born alcoholics. But once they say "I am an alcoholic" in the presence of other alcoholics, they assume a new identity. What has changed? Not so much, except how members of AA respond and, as a result, how they feel about themselves. They have moved from denying what they are and feeling alienated from others, even from themselves and their own bodies, to accepting what they have been and what they will always be even as they begin to feel like members of a new community.

Stating "I am an alcoholic" is the first move away from denial, which is the most significant impediment to success in the program. Kurtz writes of the founders early work:

> Especially in the unsuccessful phase of their efforts with drinking alcoholics, Bill and Bob had early and clearly isolated the obstacle inhibiting those who failed to grasp their ideas and so to attain so-briety—*denial*, denial fundamentally of being "an alcoholic." This denial, Wilson and Smith had learned from their failures as well as from their successes, tended to be expressed in especially two con-trary insistences: the "claim to be able to drink like other people"; and the "exceptional thinking" that insisted that even though the problem-drinker's outward experience seemed to place him in the al-coholic camp, he was somehow "different"—an exception. (59–60)

Uttering the phrase, thus, means being more honest and taking on a new identity, but it is also donning a mask that, as Flynn says, both reveals and conceals:

> Previous discussions of the identifying statement ("I'm an alcoholic") seem limited to its *revealing* qualities. In some ways, the member is

> seen as *unmasking* a part of him or herself that had previously been hidden, and as accepting the identity and role of "alcoholic." I am proposing that this phrase accomplishes, as well, the equally important task of *concealing* or *masking*. . . . It means "I am a sober alcoholic"; and for most it means "I am a sober alcoholic member of AA." By donning this "verbal mask," each speaker becomes what he or she could otherwise never be: a sober drunk. In a way, this oxymoronic label constitutes a shorthand resume, indicating the member's qualifications for speaking at the meeting. Although masks are often chosen to represent something other than the wearer, they may also be chosen to represent some particular quality actually possessed by the wearer (e.g., status, wealth, or courage). When someone chooses this latter type of mask, the single quality becomes so magnified that it effectively erases other aspects of the wearer's life and character. This, in effect, is what happens when an AA member says "I'm an alcoholic." (59)

The erasure of difference accentuates similarity and promotes objectivity, Flynn suggests. In other words, it also offers some protection: "Individual problems become almost impersonal examples of problems which, in principle, are shared by all members" (60). For those more experienced with the program, uttering the phrase becomes a verbal cue to shift into their "program mode." Flynn explains:

> I have heard gossippy [*sic*], backbiting, angry, and dishonest members suddenly shift into "program mode" and go from expressing personal indignation, privately to other members seated nearby, to extolling the virtues of acceptance, honesty, and humility in their meeting comments. It is not that one of these faces is more real than the other, but that the "masking" process taps that part of the member which is actually striving to achieve the goals of sobriety. Comments made during a meeting after such "masking" are subject to strongly felt group norms. (61)

This shift in behavior, even when not consistent with all areas of the person's life, creates a sense of membership. Of the contrast between "program mode" behavior and behavior outside of meetings, Flynn writes:

> That pre-masked members act and talk like most other people should not be surprising. Everyone, including AA members, is vulnerable to jealousy, anger, and hurt feelings. As one Oldtimer puts it, "We can never hope to rise above human being." Most AAs seem more accepting of their humanity than the rugged individuals who continue to drink. But, in the early weeks and months of recovery, as Newcomers cling to their groups as the source of strength enabling them to accomplish what they could not hope to accomplish on their own, the differences between the pre- and post-masked AA member can be extremely confusing. (62)

Newcomers might, as Flynn points out, have problems accepting the difference in how individuals act during meetings and outside meetings. She continues, "When questioned by one of her sponsees about the petty behavior of a few locally well-known anonymous Oldtimers, one Sponsor's response, through laughter, was, 'Well, what do you expect from a bunch of drunks!'" (63). Uttering the phrase does not guarantee that the speaker will behave closer to the principles and traditions of the program, but it is the first move.

"It was," Michael K. adds, "the movement toward insider status, toward the ability to participate as someone entering humanity rather than departing from it that began to heal me." His "membership in the community was renewed" each time he said the words. He began to move past self-centeredness in the new community of AA; eventually, he even found himself less isolated among his old communities—family, friends, and coworkers. Michael K. writes:

> Each time I said "I am an alcoholic," an act that was in the beginning a declaration, it seemed to count as a different illocutionary act. Even now, as I write *I am an alcoholic,* it seems to be different . . . Different—yet the same. Somehow each use of the sentence carries the memory of, the trace of, every other use of the sentence. All uses, all illocutionary forces, seem present in any one use. Thus, when I say "I am an alcoholic" in an effort to request forgiveness for drinking, I am at the same time promising to never drink again. At the same time I am asserting that I am an alcoholic, I am again declaring myself to be an alcoholic. To say repeatedly, "I am an alcoholic" is to embrace a process of becoming in order not to be. . . . I can only marvel at its power to shift its function, to aggregate in any one illocutionary act the force of all other illocutionary acts, to utterly change the life of its user. (159)

Michael K. is writing here of the multiple meanings and multiple senses of time that accumulate as the sentence is repeated. I will return to this theme several times throughout this book because it permeates the program: The transformation of identity that comes with the utterance of "I am an alcoholic" does not kill off the former self. Bill W. and Michael K. do not say, "I *used to be* an alcoholic." They say, "I *am* an alcoholic." They are the same person who used to drink; they still have the disease. But now they are a different kind of alcoholic, an alcoholic who does not drink or who has a desire to stop drinking. To say "I am an alcoholic" is not so much an act of identity as it is an act of multiple identities that would usually be separated out into different times or stages of life, a "before" self and an "after" self. It is to say "I am that former self who used to drink and did all of that alcoholic stuff," but also "I am this recovering alcoholic who is, for now, not drinking, and now is trying to live in a new way."

Saying "I am an alcoholic" is a statement of "multiple identities" (65). A single utterance of the statement carries multiple meanings, but the statement, he says, also takes on different senses with each utterance. Certainly, the speaker's intonation of the phrase changes. The first time that Michael K. said, "I am an alcoholic," his knees buckled. Was this a feeling of relief as he accepts what he had so long denied? Fear of rejection? The first awareness of what he had done during his drinking days? During his early days of the program, Michael K. probably felt one emotion and then another each time he said, "I am an alcoholic." At first, he probably felt so many different emotions at once that he had difficulty sorting them out. Eventually, as he repeats "I am an alcoholic" again and again at meetings, he finds that he can say the phrase with little emotion at all, perhaps with a sense of pride. It becomes a simple statement of fact, no different than "I have brown hair" or "I am wearing black shoes." But not entirely a simple statement of fact. With the utterance of "I am an alcoholic" eventually comes a clarity of identity and a sense of belonging. He is able to move toward acceptance of self and community with others because the members at meetings respond to his "I am an alcoholic" with "stable intonations" that "form the intonational background of a particular social group" (Bakhtin "Toward a Methodology" 166). As he repeatedly utters, "I am an alcoholic," as the audience repeatedly responds with a consistent intonation that conveys warmth and acceptance, the intonation of the response eventually transforms the utterance "I am an alcoholic." In Bakhtin's words, "the psychological aspect of the relationship of others' utterances" is eventually reflected "in the structure of the utterance itself" ("Problem of the Text" 122). The intonation of our words are changed by the intonation of the response that they receive. The "warmth" of the response to "I am an alcoholic" is typical of the "stable intonations" one encounters at AA meetings. As will be explained in more detail in the next chapter, AA meetings can be characterized as carnival, Bakhtin's term for the "other world" of open expression.

9

Carnival: A Parody of Self

> I was told in the beginning that AA stands for Altered Attitudes, and I find that that has been very important in my sobriety.
>
> —Dr. Paul O., AA Talk

> You cannot laugh and think at the same time. So every time you're laughing, you get a respite from you. And that's really important, because most of us need the break.
>
> —Ken D., AA Talk

> All historical limits are, as it were, destroyed and swept away by laughter.
>
> —M. M. Bakhtin,
> "Forms of Time and Chronotope in the Novel"

While AA does not align itself with a systematic dogma (its ninth tradition advises against opinions on "outside issues"), its groups do, nonetheless, attempt to create and reinforce a new way of thinking. In *Drinking*, Knapp describes her ambivalent reaction to the program's slogans:

> [T]he language of twelve-step programs is nothing if not repetitive, and right from the start you hear the same clichés and catchphrases and slogans over and over and over. *Don't drink, go to meetings, ask for help*: the AA mantras. *Keep it simple. One day at a time. Let go and let God.* But I welcomed the sense of brainwashing. I felt like my brain could use a good scouring out by then and I was both frightened and desperate enough to set aside whatever biases I'd brought and just listen, to absorb. I believed what I was told and I believed I belonged there, and every time I heard someone tell his story at an AA meeting, I connected with some part of it, saw a piece of myself. The people I heard at meetings also had a confidence, a calm self-acceptance, I'd coveted all my life, and I wanted what they had: serenity. (252–53)

The change in ideology that the program attempts to promote (best embodied, perhaps, in its official slogans) may strike newcomers as a form of brainwashing or, more frequently, as mere platitudes. It is the well-educated intellectual—like Knapp, educated at an Ivy League institution and a writer by profession—who tends to stumble here. It all seems a little trite. A commonly heard phrase in the program addresses this: "Some people are too smart to sober up, but no one is too stupid." Being intellectually sophisticated can be more of a detriment than an advantage. Knapp only began to accept the simple way of living expressed in the slogans because she identified with those telling their stories and she wanted what the program's ideology seemed to bring: a calmer life.

To most newcomers, like Knapp, the discourse of AA often seems like a form of brainwashing that attempts to change both behavior and thought. Newcomers are told to come to meetings, begin their days with a time of meditation, and read AA literature (reading material that is not "official" might even be discouraged, and some groups discourage the discussion of self-help books that are not part of the AA canon). Certain ideas and phrases are repeated over and over again, especially the slogans: *Let Go and Let God, Keep It Simple, One Day at a Time,* and so on. Newcomers might even be advised to repeat these, like a mantra, when under stress. More broadly stated, AA promotes a way of thinking that is more typically Eastern than Western, more paradoxical than logical (see Flynn 106–8). Ken D. says:

> It's like everything here is paradoxical. That's why when you're new, you try to apply logic. Logic is no good. Everything in AA is illogical. How do you win? You surrender. Oh, yea. But then how do I keep it? You give it away. I think I'm getting the beat. Everything's backwards. And that's what you find out about truth. If it's paradoxical, it's truthful. (AA Talk)

In AA, people certainly are encouraged to change the way they think. It all seems like propaganda: the simple phrases, the repetition, the "official" ideas. But, upon closer analysis, it seems the inverse.

The AA doctrine, if it can be called that, is expressed within a broader context of parody or carnival (see Flynn 57–58, 93–94; Nagel 42, 136). Both parody and carnival are crucial to Bakhtin's theory. In "From the Prehistory of Novelistic Discourse," Bakhtin traces the development of the novel by focusing on how one person uses the words or language of another. He begins with mimicry, "the ridiculing of another's language and another's direct discourse" (*Dialogic Imagination* 50), and then moves into diverse forms of parody, the "fourth drama" in ancient Greece that followed and satirized the tragic trilogy, the comic sermons delivered from the pulpit during holiday festivals, the satire of Rabelais, and eventually the novel. Bakhtin believes that "there never was a single strictly straightforward genre, no single type of direct discourse—artistic, rhetorical, philosophical, religious, ordinary everyday—that did not have its own parodying and travestying double, its own comic-ironic *contre-partie*" (53). In the middle ages, this parodic discourse (largely enacted through inversions, e.g., a pauper is made the mock king and then ridiculed) was even sanctioned during times of carnival, becoming a social force that opposed the stagnation of the dominant ideology. In *Rabelais and His World*, Bakhtin writes:

> As opposed to the official feast, one might say that carnival celebrated temporary liberation from the prevailing truth and from the established order; it marked the suspension of all hierarchal rank, privileges, norms, and prohibitions. . . . No dogma, no authoritarianism, no narrow-minded seriousness can coexist with Rabelaisian images; these images are opposed to all that is finished and polished, to all pomposity, to every ready-made solution in the sphere of thought and world outlook. (10, 3)

Bakhtin's analysis of carnival should not be regarded as *the* form that carnival assumes in all historical periods and all cultures. *Rabelais and His World,* written in the late 1930s in Soviet Russia, is double voiced. It is ostensibly a commentary on how carnival functioned during the late middle ages and early Renaissance in Europe, more specifically how this form of carnival is treated in the works of Rabelais; yet, it is also a commentary on Stalinist Russia (see Holquist's "Bakhtin and Rabelais," esp. 7–8). While I will argue here that AA discourse has elements of carnival, it is certainly not the carnival of Rabelais.

What AA discourse does share with Bakhtin's analysis of carnival is parody and laughter. Within the discourse of carnival, Bakhtin sees laughter as the fundamental vehicle for moving beyond static ideologies:

> Of all aspects of the ancient complex, only laughter never underwent sublimation of any sort—neither religious, mystical, nor philosophical. It never took on an official character, and even in literature the comic genres were the most free, the least regimented.
>
> After the decline of the ancient world, Europe did not know a single cult, a single ritual, a single state or civil ceremony, a single official genre or style serving either the church or the state (hymn, prayer, sacral formulas, declarations, manifestos, etc.) where laughter was sanctioned (in tone, style or language)—even in its most watered-down forms of humor and irony.
>
> Europe knew neither mysticism nor the magic of laughter, laughter was never infected, even slightly, by the "red tape" of moribund officialdom. Therefore, laughter could not be deformed or falsified as could every other form of seriousness, in particular the pathetic. Laughter remained outside official falsifications, which were coated

with a layer of pathetic seriousness. Therefore, all high and serious genres, all high forms of language and style, all mere set of phrases and all linguistic norms were drenched in conventionality, hypocrisy and falsification. Laughter alone remained uninfected by lies. ("Forms of Time" 236)

In Bakhtin's view, laughter remained apart from most literary and social traditions because of its "capability to strip . . . the object of the false verbal and ideological husk that encloses it" (237). Rabelais, Bakhtin says, found the power of laughter from "extraliterary sources," in particular, from "words and expressions connected with hard drinking" (238). While AA stories certainly do not glorify "hard drinking" (and Bakhtin would add, neither do the novels of Rabelais), there is a sense conveyed in drunk-ologs that the speaker has undergone a journey into a world apart from ordinary society—perhaps not unlike the periods of separation that make possible the visions of a Shaman—and so returns with a different per-spective on life. Speakers sees humor where most of us see pathos.

It is rather typical that members of AA or other twelve-step programs invert or parody widely accepted ideology. Dick M. mentioned, when telling his story at an AA roundup, having been institutionalized with a woman who read magazines upside down and hummed at the same time. Later in his story, he says:

> So I went to work on the twelve steps of AA, and I got to that sec-ond step. This is where I came alive and I woke up a little bit be-cause when it said "came to believe that a power greater than my-self could restore me to sanity." You know, the first thing that I thought about when it said "sanity" was me being insane. You know anybody who could get into all those scraps and mistreat all those people I did and live the horrible life I did and done all these things, hell, any insane person couldn't have done all that. You see, that was the way I was looking at it. But if I hadn't been crazy, there's no way in hell I would have done that, I'd have treated people the way I did. There's no way. And I thought about it when that word "insanity" came up. And I thought about that old gal in that sanitarium there in Memphis, when she was sitting on that couch reading that maga-zine upside down and humming all at the same time. And I got to thinking, you know, if that gal was sharp enough to read that maga-zine upside down and hum that tune, all at the same time, then I must be the sonofabitch that was crazy. (AA Talk)

Because the ideology of the broader culture is so frequently critiqued, members of twelve-step programs often speak about the inversion of "sanity" and "insanity." What they once considered sane (the way people think outside the program) they come to regard as insane. What they once thought was insane (the way people think in the program), they come to regard as sane. The inside/outside trope suggests what Bakhtin calls the "second world" of carnival, which leads to a "two-world condition" (*Rabelais and His World* 6). Within the world of carnival—the "inside" of AA meetings—the dominant ideology can be critiqued and this consciousness can be taken into everyday life—the world "outside" of AA meetings. The everyday world might remain the same, but how the individual views it has changed. Members of AA often speak of how they now laugh at situations that once made them angry or sad.

The ideas that the broader culture accepts as obviously true are also thrown into relief in more subtle ways, by mixing linguistic registers. Essential to any form of parody is the way that one language or discourse interpenetrates another. Just as, in mimicry, someone's words are repeated with a different intonation, we find, in parody, the movement of words or ideas from one language or discourse to another. This interpenetration of "styles" or languages—which Bakhtin believes to be varying forms of consciousness—creates new ways of thinking and entails a critique of dogma. Bakhtin writes:

> One who creates a direct word—whether epic, tragic or lyric—deals only with the subject whose praise he sings, or represents, or expresses, and he does so in his own language that is perceived as the sole and fully adequate tool for realizing the word's direct, objectified meaning. This meaning and the objects and themes that compose it are inseparable from the straightforward language of the person who creates it: the objects and themes are born and grow to maturity in this language, and in the national myth and national tradition that permeate this language. The position and tendency of the parodic-travestying consciousness is, however, completely different: it, too, is oriented toward the object—but toward another's words as well, a parodied word *about* the object that in the process becomes *itself* an image. Thus is created that distance between language and reality. . . . Language is transformed from the absolute dogma it had been within the narrow framework of a sealed-off and impermeable monoglossia into a working hypothesis for comprehending and expressing reality. ("From the Prehistory" 61)

As one moves from direct discourse and monoglossia to indirect discourse (someone speaking someone else's words) and polyglossia (the interpenetration of languages and, ultimately, of diverse forms of consciousness), the dogma of one language is necessarily thrown into relief by the dogma of another. Put a different way, the ideas that are so easily said in one language or discourse, even unconsciously carried along with frequently repeated expressions (a comment about a baseball game may be an unconscious endorsement of a certain economic system) may only be awkwardly said in another language and discourse. The ideas repeated unconsciously now attract attention and may even seem comic. "Only polyglossia," says Bakhtin, "fully frees consciousness from the tyranny of its own language and its own myth of language" (61).

In the rhetoric of AA, this mixing of languages most frequently occurs as the words of the former drinking self are respoken by the recovering alcoholic at an AA meeting. It can also occur as the language of different classes, regions, and institutions collide, when terms from psychology interpenetrate terms from religion or when words like "fuck" and "God" are uttered in a single sentence about the importance of living a spiritual life. When commenting on how AA is like and unlike church, Flynn writes:

> Though there is much internal debate in AA over the use of profanity in meetings, this mixture of the profane with the sacred is a hallmark of AA talk. One young man, speaking at a Las Vegas Round-up, put it this way: "I learned you could be spiritual and be a regular person too. And I learned that in meetings where I heard people say 'God' and 'fuck' in the same sentence." My first experience with this lively mixture was in 1979, when I heard an Oldtimer insist "I didn't come into AA to save my soul. I came in to save my ass. It wasn't till much later that I learned they were attached." (25)

In the spiritual program of AA, we find a bit of the barroom, more than a little cursing, and a good bit of laughing. If, as Bakhtin says, Rabelais employs the language of the marketplace in his parodies, AA talks employ the language of the barroom in theirs. Dr. Paul O. spoke of how he would, when still a newcomer, stop going to AA meetings to punish his wife, and how she decided to continue going on her own:

> She would go there by herself, just leave me at home. I don't know if . . . Have you ever tried that? Sitting at home on a Saturday night, drinking, while your non-alcoholic spouse is off laughing it up at an AA meeting? I found it boring. And I wondered what they were laughing about. I had to go back to meetings and find out. I found out that they laugh at anything. They laugh at nothing. They just laugh. And, uh . . . The problem with that was I went to meetings for seven months, and I think I went to one meeting too many, and one night I found myself laughing with them. And I haven't had a drink since. I find the laughter is very spiritual, very therapeutic. In fact, I'm convinced that my Higher Power laughs anytime he hears alcoholics or Al-Anons laugh—even if He doesn't get the joke. (AA Talk)

Dr. Paul mixes humor, spirituality, and a touch of irreverence (some might be offended by the notion that God might not "get" the joke). Ken D. makes a similar comment about miracles: "Somebody today said, 'What is the miracle of AA?' I mean there are so many miracles. I have a license. I have a checkbook. They both have the same address. And the miracle is, I live there" (AA Talk). As he mixes the language of Christianity ("miracle") with simple statements of daily routine ("I have a license"), Ken creates, as is common in the rhetoric of AA, levels of parody. He parodies the Christian notion of miracle (a miracle invokes awe: healing the sick, turning water into wine, reviving the dead) and the AA notion of miracle (a miracle is attaining a new life: sobriety, serenity, friends, family) in the same way that he parodies his former self (the practicing alcoholic who could not keep a license or a checkbook or a domicile), and all this circles back to the speaker himself to parody his position of authority. We usually think of the speaker as an authority, one who knows more than the audience and one who will deliver the truth. Certainly, speakers in most contexts attempt to create and maintain a sense of authority. In AA talks, the speaker's authority, which comes from his lived experience as an alcoholic and his membership in AA, is played against a parody of self, which Bakhtin says is typical of carnival. The speaker's authority, in other words, is created through self-effacement, by aligning oneself with the program.

During the carnivalistic moments of AA stories, the voice of the speaker is similar to the narrative voice of the novel, which derives, Bakhtin says, from the folk figures of the fool, clown, and rogue. Bakhtin says that this voice, a mask that the novelist wears as narrator, is "rooted deep in the folk" and "linked to the fool's time-honored privilege not to participate in life, and by the time-honored bluntness of the fool's language" ("Forms of Time" 161). His description is similar to Jung's archetype of the trickster, which also inverts conventional values (see "On the Psychology of the Trickster Figure" in *The Archetypes and the Collective Unconscious* [*Collected Works*] 255–72). Bakhtin says:

> Essential to these three figures is a distinctive feature that is as well a privilege—the right to be "other" in this world, the right not to make common cause with any single one of the existing categories that life makes available; none of these categories quite suits them, they see the underside and the falseness of every situation. Therefore, they can exploit any position they choose, but only as a mask. The rogue still has some ties that bind him to real life; the clown and the fool, however, are "not of this world," and therefore possess their own special rights and privileges. These figures are laughed at by others, and *themselves* as well. Their laughter bears the stamp of the public square where the folk gather. They re-establish the public nature of the human figure: the entire being of characters such as these is, after all, utterly on the surface; everything is brought out on to the square. . . . This creates that distinctive means for externalizing a human being, via parodic laughter. ("Forms of Time" 159–60)

This voice has a "transforming influence" that has the task of "the laying-bare of any sort of conventionality, the exposure of all that is vulgar and falsely stereotyped in human relationships" (160, 162). As V. L. Makhlin has argued, Bakhtin's laughter—a "laughing outsideness"—is one of the "visible forms and roots of dialogism" (qtd. in Emerson 196). When speakers laugh at themselves as others do, they can begin to see themselves as others consummate them (196). Laughter, especially as part of self-parody, humbles the self and connects the self with others. One speaker recalled how she was unable to laugh about an embarrassing situation in her life. She spoke about it at an AA meeting, with tears, when her daughter was in the audience. Then she overheard her daughter retelling the story to friends, all of whom saw it as humorous. It was only at this point, when she saw her experience through the eyes of others, that she was able to see the humor in it and move past her guilt. This exteriorizing of self, which in AA talks often happens at the moment when one begins to tell his or her story as a parody of self, is a crucial point in recovery. It moves the speaker past guilt and paves the way for communion.

Certainly, moments of discourse of AA can be viewed as a form of carnival, a parodic-travestying double of the ideology that barrages us daily in conversation, advertising, political speeches, educational lectures, and sermons. It also has single-voiced moments, when members speak of the "program" and its ideas. These moments might be viewed as monologic if viewed out of context. Indeed, some critics have used such moments to argue that AA is an authoritarian organization that rigidly enforces certain ways of thinking. But these single-voiced moments are not so much "preached" as "shared," not so much in the sense of "you must" as "this is what worked for me, maybe it will work for you." Even the ideology and shared experience of AA is questioned in the most reverent of moments. When telling his story at an AA picnic, at the point in his story when speakers typically express their gratitude to AA, Ted H. said:

> In Alcoholics Anonymous, and I have to say this is the first time I've ever shared this, and I had pondered it many times today, but, because it's the truth and it might be meaningful to somebody else, that I have suffered the greatest personal attacks and the greatest indignities ever done to me in my life inside Alcoholics Anonymous, you know, but I have suffered the least from them of any other time in my life. (AA Talk)

Most speakers comment on the gifts of their "fellowship": They find a more serene life and loyal friends. Here, Ted raises some questions about these common beliefs, even as he acknowledges his debt to the program.

When the single-voiced moments are not overtly challenging AA ideology, they are implicitly challenged because they always occur in a broader dialogic context. At topic meetings, for example, members take turns discussing some topic (e.g., acceptance, letting go, etc.). During these meetings, there is a prohibition on cross talk. In other words, when a

member speaks, others are not allowed to interrupt and directly comment on what he or she is saying. Think of how this is different from
ordinary conversation. John, for example, may tell his friend Susan that
he feels bad about something that happened at work. He wants to express his feelings and be heard. Susan, feeling that she is being a good,
attentive listener, interrupts and asks, "What did he say then?" Or "Why
did you do that?" John becomes frustrated with telling his story. Susan
might even take over the story: "The same thing happened to me just
yesterday. . . ." Or she may stop the speaker to offer advice: "You know
what you should do? . . ." John becomes angry. He didn't want to be
interrupted; he didn't want advice. He only wanted a silent audience to
hear him without comment. After feeling alienated from others at work,
he wants to feel reconnected with his friends. In topic meetings, in contrast to ordinary conversation, speakers express themselves and others listen
without comment. The meeting is seemingly a series of monologues. Certainly, the members learn from what others say as they draw conclusions
from how their monologues are situated among others, but there is a sense
that each person is allowed to express himself or herself and is heard.

At times, the discourse of AA approaches the single voiced without
the power issues of the monologic. While the broader context remains
dialogic, voices begin to be sorted out. While I am unaware of Bakhtin
describing a process similar to what I am here calling the "sorting out of
voices," he does discuss how we internalize authoritative voices that then
become "innerly persuasive voices." We can achieve some freedom from
these voices through parody. Morson and Emerson write:

> Much as authoritative discourses may come to lose their authority,
> so innerly persuasive discourses can some to seem less persuasive,
> *more* than half "someone else's." When this happens, we typically
> begin to play with the discourse, make an objectified image of it, turn
> it into a "word of the second type," or attach it to a specific other
> person one holds at some distance. One investigates it from various
> perspectives in order to understand its limitations. One may begin
> to stylize or even parody the formerly persuasive voice. (222)

From parody, single voices emerge. In confessional moments, when
speakers admit some wrong to another human being, or expressive moments, when they share their emotional pain, there is but one voice in the
room. In *Drinking*, Knapp describes one such moment:

> During my first year a woman at a meeting raised her hand and said
> that her brother had died very suddenly of a brain aneurysm several
> days earlier. The woman was still shell-shocked and disbelieving but
> she talked for about five minutes about what it was like to get
> through this experience without a drink, about how painful it was

but also how grateful she felt to be *present,* available to her family, capable of feeling the full range of emotions that accompany such experiences.

When people talk like that about their deepest pain, a stillness often falls over the room, a hush that's so deep and so deeply shared it feels like reverence. That stillness keeps me coming, and it helps keep me sober, reminding me what it means to be alive to emotion, what it means to be human. (256)

Such experiences perhaps feel even more genuine given that they emerge from a discourse that is more characterized by carnival—the comic and the parodic. In a room where people are laughing one moment and crying the next, there is less pressure to "bullshit" others. It is carnival that makes communion possible. And perhaps there is a sense that people really listen because they have been relieved of the responsibility of responding, which might take many forms (condolences, advice, denials) but that have a similar effect, a shift of attention from the speaker to the auditor.

10

Taking On a New Identity: Faking It to Make It

> When I don't go to meetings, I have a habit of forgetting. And I think of myself as separate. But, when I do go to meetings, I remember. Meetings help me to remember. And the way I look at that word "remember" is that I'm a member again, I'm active, I'm doing the things I need to do.
>
> —Ken D., AA Talk

> There are two kinds of people to watch in A.A.—those who make it, and those who don't.
>
> —Ernie G., *Dr. Bob and the Good Oldtimers*

It is a common expression of old-timers that they either did not know themselves as they were coming of age or that they lost their identities as their drinking progressed. Caroline Knapp describes bottoming out—while she was trying to manage, without much success, two separate relationships—as losing touch with her social role:

> Denial—first of drinking, then of the self—stretches to include more and more bits of reality, and after a while you literally cannot see the truth, cannot see your own role in the disaster you've made of your life, cannot see who you are or what you need or what choices you have. During that period, juggling both relationships, my life took on a deeply fragmented quality, with different personæ emerging and becoming more distinct and also more false. (206–7)

As Knapp says, "drinking interferes with the larger, murkier business of *identity*, of forming a sense of self as strong and capable and aware" (80). Of their early days in AA, members often say that they discover who they are. They might say, for example, "I found who I really am in here. Before I came to AA, I didn't know who I was." This is part of the process of "sorting out the voices" within the carnival context of AA meetings, but newcomers take on an identity in other ways as well.

The search for identity within AA might seem to be the kind of interior psychological journey that is historically associated with the Romantics: The individual goes within and discovers his or her true self. But taking on a new identity within AA has much more to do with the persona, a person's social role.[1] C. G. Jung described the persona as a mask that we wear in public:

> Fundamentally the persona is nothing real: it is a compromise between individual and society as to what a man should appear to be. He takes a name, earns a title, exercises a function, he is this or that. In a certain sense all this is real, yet in relation to the essential individuality of the person concerned it is only a secondary reality, a compromise formation, in making which others often have a greater share than he. The persona is a semblance, a two-dimensional reality, to give it a nickname. (Collected Works 7: 158)

It is through acting out a persona, playing a role—usually one that is already historically present, handed to us by our culture—that we establish our social identity. This sense of identity might be quite different from that of the ego, what we consider ourselves to be when we reflect upon our thoughts and actions. As Jung explains it, an individual's consciousness is in a constant state of flux, flowing outward into a persona (becoming lost, if only momentarily, in a social role) and flowing back to the ego during reflective moments (when we evaluate, among other things, our investment in our persona: Am I really this role that I play, or am I something different?). For more psychologically healthy individuals, the persona and the ego are not so far apart as they serve the role of mediating the needs of the individual and his or her adaptation to the norms of society. For the less psychologically healthy individual, the flow of consciousness takes on the character of flight or denial. We flee into a persona, because we cannot bear the shame and guilt that we feel as we reflect on who we really are. We flee from the persona into the ego to deny our acts; I am not, we say, the kind of person who does these things. Not surprisingly for alcoholics, this flight is more exaggerated and leads to detachment. Alcoholics often describe bottoming out as the phase when they seem out of their own bodies, viewing their actions as if they were watching the movements of another person.

Both the Oxford Group and early AAs considered the deflation of an unrealistic sense of self to be a crucial step in the establishment of a new identity and a revitalized relationship with God. When AA was still known as the "alcoholic squad" of the Oxford Group in Akron, which then met in the home of T. Henry and Clarace Williamson, members would take a newcomer upstairs to force a surrender to God:

> Dorothy S.M. recalled the 1937 meetings when "the men would all disappear upstairs and all of us women would be nervous and worried about what was going on. After about half an hour or so, down would come the new man, shaking, white, serious, and grim. And all the people who were already in A.A. would come trooping down after him. They were pretty reluctant to talk about what had happened, but after a while, they would tell us they had had a *real* surrender."[2] (*Dr. Bob* 101)

Bill W. recollected how he and Dr. Bob poured "the medical hopelessness" of alcoholism into Bill D., their first real success, how "that lowered him down two notches" until "he was like a meatball" and "didn't seem to bounce" (AA Talk).[3] Bill W. later explained this process in a December 15, 1950, letter to Clarian S. He wrote that most "human woes seem to be caused by ego demands" and that even "social theorists" seem to encourage "ego-feeding." He continues:

> Now A.A. doesn't work on that basis at all. Every Step, every Tradition, takes a healthy swap at careening egos. The very first Step is a sockdologer. Far from being sufficient, it says the drunk hasn't any power at all on his own. If anything, A.A. is practical; it works. The process is ego-deflation and dependence upon a Higher Power. Moreover, the process is working upon terrible misshapen egos. The social result is pretty good. Good enough so that the outside world is being hold [*sic*] up as an example. Paradoxically, we are getting strong by deflation.

In most current AA groups, contrary to the practice of AA when it was still associated with the Oxford Group, this deflation of identity is a slower process; it occurs as members work the steps with their sponsors or have their beliefs challenged at topic meetings; it is not forced upon the individual by the group at the newcomer's first meeting.

As the persona of the practicing alcoholic is discarded, which begins with the first utterance of "I am an alcoholic," a newcomer moves from thinking that he or she is one of the most important individuals in the world—remember that Bill W. likened his alcoholic self to Napoleon when his drinking was most severe—to a sense of humility. In AA, one often hears the comment: "I am not very important." Speakers even typically deny that they have "authored" their own stories. Dick M. said: "Before I get into saying anything, let me get it straight and say it now, whatever I say and whatever I know, whatever I've learned and whatever I am came from this program of Alcoholics Anonymous, cause I learned it from somebody else" (AA Talk). If the speaker has any wisdom, it comes from God or the program. This humility and mitigation of the importance of the individual, the first moment in recovery, becomes an enduring trait of the persona one adopts in the program.

In this sense, one learns how to act in AA from the outside (by seemingly playing a game) to the inside (by eventually identifying with the role that one plays in meetings). Ted H. says:

> I started permanent sobriety October 1st of 1986, but I'd had a year or so of experience with Alcoholics Anonymous previous to that. And when I became a member of Alcoholics Anonymous, when I started just virtually imitating what you guys did, eventually it went from my head to my heart. And finally one day I was able to say to myself that I'm not alone anymore, that these people have the same sets of fears and doubts. They had the same "colossal failure" in their lives that I had in mine. (AA Talk)

One frequently hears old-timers advise newcomers to "fake it" or "pretend to be better." It is through action and acting—a form of play—that newcomers take on a new identity in the program.

Jung, Vygotsky, and Bakhtin all acknowledge the importance of play. For Bakhtin, play and art, which is play with a spectator, allow us to develop "sympathetic co-experience," the objectification of self and the subjectification of the "Other." This is how Bakhtin describes an actor's creation of a *dramatic persona:*

> The artistic image of the hero is created by the actor before a mirror, before a director, on the basis of his own stock of experience. This process of creation involves makeup (even if the actor is made up by someone else, he still takes makeup into account as an aesthetically significant constituent of the image of the hero); demeanor; the form given to various movements and positions of the body in relation to other objects and to the background; training of the voice as heard and evaluated from outside; and, finally, the creation of character (character as an artistic constituent is transgredient to the consciousness of the one who is characterized, as we shall soon see). And all this is done by the actor in association with the artistic whole of the play (and not the event of the hero's life); in this context, the actor *is* an artist. In this context, the actor's aesthetic self-activity is directed to giving human form to a human being as hero and to giving form to his life. When, on the other hand, the actor, in playing his role, "reincarnates" *himself* in the hero, then all these constituents of forming the hero from outside become transgredient to the actor's consciousness and experiencing *as* the hero (let us assume that the "reincarnation" is accomplished in its purest form). The form of the body as shaped from the outside, its movements and positions, etc.— all these constituents will have artistic validity only for the conscious-

> ness of a contemplator—*within the artistic whole* of the play, not
> within the experienced life of the hero. ("Author and Hero" 77)

Newcomers take on the program by playing out a new role that is, in a
sense, taking on the identity of the founders—Bill W. and Dr. Bob—and
the identity of the old-timers who embody the traditions of AA. This is
not to say that one's "individuality" is erased (indeed, members often
speak of finding their "true" selves within the program), but there is
certainly a sense that newcomers must identify with other alcoholics if
they are to stay sober. O'Reilly writes:

> Since speakers aspire to exemplify recovery, to validate program
> principles and emblematize "success" to the audience, idiosyncra-
> sies that could interfere with identification may be flattened; incidents
> may be screened against a potentially damaging effect. Extension and
> universalization are weighed against the particularities of that which
> is entirely private. The program "message" of hope is superior in
> value to historical truth—but this notion co-exists with the ideal of
> honesty, so that representations must be carefully, deliberately me-
> diated. (*Sobering Tales* 158)

When telling his story, Dr. Paul O. directed these comments to the newcomers in the audience:

> You may even feel that this [program] is okay for us but certainly
> not something for you. It just doesn't seem to fit your needs. Or,
> especially if you feel your case is different. The bad news about you
> feeling your case is different, the bad news is that that makes you
> one of us. Because that is how you get here—by being different. If
> you think you're different, you're right. Look around the room. You
> won't find anybody here who looks just like you. There never has
> been anybody just . . . we're all different. No two of us are the same.
> We're all just little snowflakes. [Ironically] Ahhh. We were saying
> this weekend, if there are two of us exactly alike, then one of us
> would be unnecessary. So we are different. But the point is, we are
> more alike than we are different. You can either spend the rest of
> your life looking at the similarities, or looking at the differences. If
> you look for the similarities, you'll probably stay sober. And, if you
> focus on the differences, you'll probably continue to drink. (AA Talk)

Within AA, at least initially, it is crucial that the newcomer identify with
others, begin to move beyond a sense that no one else in the world has "my
kind of problems," no one else "has done the things that I have done."
As they identify with others in the program, newcomers take on a new
persona (they learn how to talk "program talk" in what typically seems,
to the old-timers, to be a rather bad playacting). Even when they are not
advised to do so, they try to play a role that they do not yet understand.
The old-timers respond by saying, "Keep coming back." The phrase has

more than one meaning. It means what it literally states: "We want you to keep coming to meetings." Or it can, on occasion, mean something else: "You haven't got it yet. Keep coming back until you understand the program." It is usually only the old-timers who understand it in this sense. In the early days of sobriety, newcomers seem to "fake it," in part because they do not yet understand the role and the program but also because they are *only* playing a role. They have not yet done the discovery work—explored their unique history and discovered their "inner selves"—that provides texture and depth to the role, a style of playing the role, and, at times, a resistance to the role. The discovery work is accomplished by working Steps Four through Nine. By the time most people have finished the ninth step, they no longer sense they are "faking" it. Old-timers, who have thoroughly worked the steps, speak out of the persona of the program, but they also comment on how their experiences differs from Bill W.'s story or the typical story of other alcoholics.

But what exactly is this new persona? This might best be answered by first describing what it is not. To provide an example, I will need to step out of the AA culture and literature and cite a passage from Frederick Exley's *A Fan's Notes*. The book, by the author's claim, is a fictionalized autobiography. Exley's persona, a practicing alcoholic and a rather unenthusiastic high school teacher, describes his students as being nearly subhuman:

> The curriculum was, as it had been in the two schools where I had substituted, as bland as hominy grits; and there was a faculty that might most kindly be referred to as not altogether cretinous. A freshman had nuns cloistered in a "Beanery," a sophomore thought the characters in *Julius Caesar* talked "pretty damn uppity for a bunch of Wops," a junior defined "in mufit" as the attire worn by "some kind of sexual freak (like a certain ape who sits a few seats from me!)," and a senior considered "Hamlet a fag if I ever saw one. I mean, yak, yak, yak, instead of sticking that Claude in the gizzard, that Claude who's doing all those smelly things to his Mom." (3)

Throughout the autobiography/novel, the Exley persona parodies (Bakhtin would call this double-voiced discourse that is unidirectional and passive) everyone around him, and he is extremely good at pointing to the faults of others. Essentially, Exley takes the words of another and places a new value on them as they become subsumed by his own voice. It is double voiced because we hear the students' voices (if only highly distorted) through Exley's voice. It is unidirectional because Exley's voice changes the meaning and value of the students' voices, but they do not change the meaning or value of his voice (see Morson and Emerson 149–52). In passages in which the narrator moves the focus to his own sense of self, Exley celebrates his bohemian antics, but the acts of a persona who is seemingly too good for American culture only thinly disguise an intense self-loathing. O'Reilly argues that Exley wears "a mask of docility" that protects "the damaged but still-precious self" (*Sobering Tales* 90). Throughout the work, the reader moves from moments of being amused by Exley's antics and his disdain of those around him to sadness about the conditions of his deteriorating life; such shifts mirror the mood swings of practicing alcoholics. In the following passage, he describes his Sundays of drinking and watching football at his favorite bar:

> The choice of The Parrot as a place to view the games was not an arbitrary one. There had been a time, some two or three seasons before, when I had been able to bounce up and down—shouting, "Oh, God, he did it! Gifford did it! He caught the goddam thing!"— in any place, in any company, and feel neither the timidity nor embarrassment. But as one year had engulfed another, and still another, each bringing with it its myriad defeats, as I had come to find myself relying on the Giants as a life-giving, an exalting force, I found myself unable to relax in the company of "unbelievers," in the company of those who did not take their football earnestly or who thought my team something less than the One God. At those times, in those alien places, I felt like a holy man attempting to genuflect amidst a gang of drunken, babbling, mocking heretics. I tried a number of places in Watertown before settling on The Parrot; though it was not exactly the cathedral I would have wished for, it was—like certain old limestone churches scattered throughout the north country—not without its quaint charms. It was ideally isolated on a hill above the city; sitting at the bar I was seldom aware of the city's presence, and when I was, I could think of it as a nostalgic place beneath me, a place with elm trees and church towers and bone-clean streets; sitting at the bar, the city could be thought of as a place remembered, and remembered as if from a distance. (8–9)

There is something like this in many stories told in AA. Speakers talk of the "drinking days," of their inflated personæ playing counterpoint to a deep sense of shame, needing to find a place where one felt accepted even if also terribly alone, apart from the gaze of nonalcoholics. Indeed, the leitmotif of *A Fan's Notes*, it might be argued, is the search for a place of comfort—beyond judgment and shame—even if in this place Exley is also lost in lies, lost in a crowd, without friends. All this might be part of the drunkolog of an AA story, except, in Exley's story, the author and the hero (his "fictionalized" persona) are all too close.

In AA stories, especially those told by old-timers, there is a distance. The author (the speaker, the present self, the recovering alcoholic) parodies rather than celebrates the acts of a former drunken self as contrasting identities clash (the deluded drinker and the recovering alcoholic). And, despite the confession of acts that most of us would rationalize, brush aside, or deny, there is not a sense of shame—all of which could not happen without humor. In the following passage, Dr. Paul O. recounts how he was forced into craft projects when on the "nut ward" of a hospital where he, as a physician, was on staff:

> They tried to convince me that the quality of my life would be improved if I learned how to make leather belts. I just . . . It made no sense. I told them, "I have a whole wall covered with licenses and certificates and diplomas and papers to prove that I had been educated way beyond my level of intelligence. And I don't see how making leather belts will improve my life in any way." And besides they don't understand the instructions. That wasn't my fault. That was the fault of some Occupational Therapist. Cause I've always had the theory that if you don't understand a thing well enough that you can explain it to me so I can understand it, then you don't understand it as well as you're supposed to. And she'd already explained it three times. I wasn't going to embarrass her by asking her a fourth time. (AA Talk)

Dr. Paul's former self criticizes others (much in the way that Exley's persona criticizes his students, his wife, his lovers, his friends, his boss, etc.), but this former self is parodied by Dr. Paul's present self. Typical of the drunkolog section of AA talks, we see multiple voices that represent "concrete reference-points," each a separate consciousness (Bakhtin, *Toward a Philosophy* 66). Drunkologs are filled with implied quotation marks (shifts in the intonation of the speaker's voice to denote the voice of another) and markers of other voices: *he said, she said, they said*. These other voices, which were once marginalized in a monologic battle or regarded with indifference, come back to life in a parodic moment. For old-timers, the drunkolog becomes a means of making amends to the voices that the speaker once stifled.

We do not find this clash of identities in Exley's narrative. When Exley's persona criticizes and blames others, the reader senses that Exley believes the persona is right—his students *are* stupid, his wife *is* difficult, his boss *is* moronic. The reader laughs with Exley *at* the people around him. In contrast, when Dr. Paul's former self blames the occupational therapist for not knowing how to make a leather belt, the listener knows that he is really parodying his former self for blaming others. The listener laughs with the present Dr. Paul *at* the former Dr. Paul. When he relates what "he told them" (the comments about having "licenses and certificates and diplomas and papers"), Dr. Paul is employing what Bakhtin calls indirect speech and so is producing an active "double-voiced" discourse.[4] He is taking words spoken in one context (a psych ward) and repeating them with a contrasting tone in another context (an AA meeting). These words, which his former self spoke with great pride to the occupational therapist, are now said again in a different intonation, the higher pitch of Dr.

Paul's voice. We also hear the voice of the occupational therapist. While she is the object of parody within the voice of Dr. Paul's former self, she is, within the overarching voice of Dr. Paul's present self, the agent of parody against Dr. Paul's former self. Further, since the present Dr. Paul identifies with his former self, the multiple voices (and the multiple parodies) are also directed, to some degree, to the voice of the speaker.

The effect of one voice undoing another, as Bakhtin repeatedly says, effects a shift in power relations. In the anecdote about his days in treatment, Dr. Paul is a physician on staff with the hospital at which he was a patient. He attempted to maintain his position (as a physician) over that of the occupational therapist, who asserts her authority over him (as patient). The occupational therapist's attempts to force Dr. Paul to make a leather belt is monologic, as is, of course, Dr. Paul's attempts to play the role of physician when wearing a bathrobe. When the event is narrated, as Dr. Paul parodies his former inflated persona, all moves toward power seem silly: The monologic battle between Dr. Paul and the occupational therapist respoken as part of an AA story becomes dialogic.

In contrast to Exley's narrative, Dr. Paul seems to speak without shame, without some dark, underlying sense of self-loathing. A later passage of his talk, when Dr. Paul shares a parable about entering heaven, gives a sense of his ethos:

> If we do have a pre-admission interview with St. Peter before we get in, he's not going to ask if we've been good or bad. I think he's going to say, "What was your predominant mood or attitude down there?" "What do you want me to say, 'Guilty?'" "No," he will say, "I know you've heard a lot about . . . we're not nearly as obsessed with guilt as you think, but I know that you know that this is a place of happiness, peace and joy. What you don't know is how we keep it that way. Unhappy, resentful, complaining, whining, victims, bad people, there's a special place for them. In fact, you're standing over the trap door. With that in mind, what was your predominant mood down there?" (AA Talk)

Typical of the talks of so many old-timers, Dr. Paul's talk of June 1995, performed when he had been in the program twenty-seven years, was filled with humor from beginning to end. There is no wallowing in guilt or shame, despite the content of the story.

How is it that Dr. Paul, and other AA speakers, are able to achieve this ethos—to become more comfortable with their senses of self, their egos? How are they able to move beyond guilt and shame? As we will see in the next chapter, they do so through acts of confession.

11

Confessional Self-Accounting: Speaking *Before* Rather Than *To* an Audience

> Self-objectification (in the lyric, in the confession, and so forth) as self-alienation and, to a certain degree, a surmounting of the self. By objectifying myself (i.e., by placing myself outside) I gain the opportunity to have an authentically dialogic relation with myself.
>
> —M. M. Bakhtin, "The Problem of the Text"

In his description of confessional self-accounting, Bakhtin writes of how "one's soul could look exactly the way one's face looks" when possessed "by the mirrored image of oneself" ("Author and Hero" 146). The phrase (being possessed by a "mirrored image") is meant to convey the way that one sees one's self through the eyes of others. Of Bakhtin's system, Patterson writes: "[T]he I comes to itself by way of the other" (56). Clark and Holquist write:

> [I]f my deepest self, my I-for-myself, is in essence opposed to all categories, the question arises as to where I am to get the categories for fixing the self itself. The answer is: from other selves. I cannot see the self that is my own, so I must try to perceive it in others' eyes. This process of conceptually seeing myself by refracting the world through values of the other begins very early, when children first begin to see themselves through the eyes of their mother, and it continues all their lives. (73)

If we see in others only displeasure and blame, as they direct their gazes toward us, as their faces become for us a mirror, our faces react with a grimace and we begin to feel shame and self-hatred. Then as we speak, we lapse into perversions of confessional self-accounting (resentment, cynicism, irony, defiance, and invectives) that function as a defense against the judgments of others. Of the invective, a "confessional self-accounting turned inside out," Bakhtin writes:

> The tendency of this worst kind of invective or abuse is to tell the
> other what he alone can and *must* say of himself—to "cut him to
> the quick." The worst kind of invective is the just invective, which
> expresses in tones of malice and mockery what the other himself
> could say about himself in penitential-petitionary tones. . . . ("Au-
> thor and Hero" 146)

Most of us are familiar with this kind of perversion of confessional self-
accounting: the criticizing of oneself, the criticizing of others, cynicism
of others' motives, the ironic admission that is no admission at all, resentment about how others treat one, and playing the fool.

It is true confessional self-accounting, rather than these perversions,
Bakhtin says, that leads to spiritual growth. He describes it thus:

> In confessional self-accounting, there is no hero and there is no au-
> thor, for there is no position for actualizing their interrelationship,
> no position of being axiologically situated outside it. Author and hero
> are fused into one: it is the spirit prevailing over the soul in process
> of its own becoming, and finding itself unable to achieve its own
> completion or consummation, except for a certain degree of consoli-
> dation that it gains, through anticipation, in God (the spirit that has
> become naive). In confessional self-accounting, there is not a single
> constituent that is self-sufficient and disengaged from the unitary and
> unique event of being. . . . (147)

Bakhtin characterizes confessional self-accounting as an act rather than
an artistic creation. It is spontaneously performed, and it achieves a degree of sincerity, in its purer forms, because it is ultimately an accounting of oneself to oneself before God. It is *not* like the sideward glance,
the kind of speech acts found in "Notes from the Underground," or perversions of confessional self-accounting, which are directed toward the
"mirrored image" on the faces of those around us.

If confessional self-accounting, which forms the spiritual core of AA
stories, takes us away from the everyday discourse that anticipates a negative reaction, how is it different? Bakhtin writes that confession "is a
self-objectification" from which "the *other* with his special, *privileged*
approach is excluded." The "organizing principle," he continues, "is the
pure relationship of the *I* to itself" (142). For the confessional self-accounting to remain an *act* rather than a crafted work of art, it needs a
special audience:

> Pure, solitary self-accounting is impossible; the nearer a self-account-
> ing comes to this ultimate limit, the clearer becomes the other ulti-
> mate limit, the action of the other ultimate limit; the deeper the soli-
> tude (value-related solitude) with oneself, and, consequently, the
> deeper the repentance and the passing-beyond-oneself, the clearer
> and more essential is one's referredness to God. In an absolute

axiological void, no utterance is possible, nor is consciousness itself possible. Outside God, outside the bounds of trust in absolute otherness, self-consciousness and self-utterance are impossible, and they are impossible not because they would be senseless practically, but because trust in God is an immanent constitute moment of pure self-consciousness and self-expression. . . . A certain degree of warmth is needed in the value-related atmosphere that surrounds me, in order that my self-consciousness and my self-utterance could actualize themselves in it, in order that life could commence. The mere fact that I attach any significance at all to my own determinateness (even if it is an infinitely negative significance), the mere fact that I bring it up at all for discussion, that is, the very fact of becoming conscious of myself in being, testifies in itself that I am not alone in my self-accounting, that someone is interested in me, that someone wants me to be good. (144)

Bakhtin speaks here of the setting, the rhetorical situation, that makes confessional self-accounting possible: faith and trust in God and, ultimately, faith and trust in others. Certainly, a central part of the program is coming, as Bill W. wrote of his own conversion, to a new relationship with God, which should carry over into a new relationship with others.

It is, perhaps, the second part of this process, developing trust in others, that is most difficult. How do cynical people come to trust others? The culture of AA as a whole contributes to this process. The first confession that all members make ("I am an alcoholic") is met with acceptance and, so, opens the way to other confessions. The talk of spirituality, the inclusion of prayer into meetings, and the focus on personal growth contribute to the creation of an atmosphere in which confession is easier. The tradition of anonymity, of prohibitions against "cross talk" and gossip, of hugs and the phrase "glad you're here" give the sense of a safe environment, what Bakhtin calls "warmth." The example of the old-timers demonstrates that one can be honest without being judged. Most importantly, the members of AA are all alcoholics. They felt stigmatized in their community; now they are among other alcoholics. A sense develops that "we" are all alike, that someone has already confessed what the speaker is about to say.

What does it mean to confess to others who have done everything that you have been ashamed to confess, maybe even to yourself? When newcomers begin the fourth step (the "searching and fearless moral inventory"), they often express concern to their sponsors about saying how they have harmed others and themselves (as they will in the fifth step, where they admit "to God, to ourselves, and to another human being the exact nature of our wrongs"). The sponsor usually says something like, "I have either done it or heard it all before." Newcomers soon find that it is difficult—maybe impossible—to shock their sponsors or other members of AA. The unsayable is heard in a way that levels it with other statements. "I stole from my boss" evokes no more of a response than "It is sunny today."[1]

When speakers are in a moment of confessional self-accounting, they have to trust the audience. They learn to trust the audience because the others before them have been there. The acceptance by the audience in the general culture of AA makes the confession possible, but once *in* the act of confession, the audience seems to disappear. When in the mode of confessional self-accounting, whether in a speaker meeting or a topic meeting, speakers seem unaware of the audience. They do not look directly at the audience; they may even be unaware that some of the audience are speaking among themselves. These confessional moments are often narrated without details or context ("I've lied to many people," "I harmed my children," or "I was not a good friend"), vaguely alluded to ("Something happened at work this week"), or suggested by a series of comments that remain unconnected. The sequence of narrative time disappears, almost as if the events happen apart from time. Speakers may seem in a trance, feeling lost in time as they now experience feelings about past events. Only the speakers themselves may connect the act of confession with any biographical content. The audience may know only the affect of the confession, how speakers feel about their past behaviors, and be at an absolute loss to know what actually happened. When these confessional moments occur, speakers are not asked to supply more details. There is no sense that the audience needs to understand in a biographical or historical sense what happened.

While doing the fifth step, members do confess to their sponsors the actual content of their past actions, but within the context of a speaker meeting, confession is more of a vague reference. Lisa B., for example, described her bottoming out in this way:

> I had to do a few more months of exploring, and what my bottom was . . . was, um, that I . . . I became the absolute worst person that I thought I could be. Every moral and ideal that I had ever set or that my Mom had helped me to set in my life, I had went against. Everything that I knew that was right, I had disregarded. And what happened in the end was I was drinking . . . why I stopped drinking . . . and I'll tell you why I stopped drinking. I stopped drinking about two weeks before I went into treatment. And that was because my last drunk I did a lot of horrible things and there are a lot of angry, very hurt people. And, uh, once again I had people looking at me and shaking me and saying, "Why?" You know, "Why are you like you are and why do you do the things you do?" And once again, I really didn't know. I mean, I really didn't know. When people would ask me that, I had no idea why. Um, it might sound like a copout, but it was true. So my bottom was that I became the absolute worst

person and, uh, worse than that was I couldn't stop. It was no longer
a choice of, "Oh, a few months here, I'll just taper off and go to the
next state and change lives all over again." (AA Talk)

Lisa refers to breaking every moral that she had ever established, but then
she stops. She does not say in detail what these morals were or what she
did to break them. She only confesses in the sense that she says enough
for her to know that she is connecting with her past actions and is acknowledging before God and other members of AA that she remembers
and regrets these actions, but she is also saying, "The details of what I
did are none of your business." As she withdraws from narrative elaboration, she establishes a boundary. When the audience does not ask her
to say more, they say, in effect, that they respect that boundary.

Artistic narrative often hinges on details because authors (writers or
speakers) serve the audience. Authors attempt to capture a moment of
their lives, shape it into autobiography, or create a world in fiction that
the audience can recreate in their imaginations. If the narrative is poorly
crafted, the audience reacts by throwing rotten fruit, booing, or leaving
the theater, throwing down the book, or critiquing the text. Even the more
polite audiences shift restlessly in their seats, yawn, and sigh. In short, if
the audience feels poorly served, they distance themselves from the author. In AA narratives, especially those with confessional moments, the
process is reversed: The audience serves the speaker. This is most apparent when the speaker is boring. What typically happens on these occasions is the audience sits and listens with reverence. They usually do not
talk or shift in their seats or roll their eyes. If anything, the audience seems
more quiet than usual, more attentive and respectful. It is extremely rare
for someone to leave early. When the speaker makes a rather poor attempt at humor, the audience laughs. When he or she finishes, the audience applauds. Individuals give the speaker a hug and compliment the
talk. They are not just being nice. The audience benefits even from talks
that seem entirely self-absorbed because they sense that they have been
of service to one of their own as that person, or someone else, will some-
day be of service to them.

The audience is playing a rather odd role here. In confessional moments, speakers are not speaking *to the audience* but are speaking to themselves *before the audience*. Paradoxically, the audience is only important
to demonstrate that they are not important at all. Bakhtin writes:

> [T]he *other* may be needed as a judge who must judge me the way I
> judge myself, without aestheticizing me; he may be needed in order
> to destroy his possible influence upon my self-evaluation, that is, in
> order to enable me, by way of self-abasement before him, to liber-
> ate myself from that possible influence exerted by his valuating po-
> sition outside me and the possibilities associated with this position

(to be unafraid of the opinion of others, to overcome my fear of shame). ("Author and Hero" 142)

As alcoholics confess their most hidden secrets to their higher power and other alcoholics, the secrets begin to lose power. This is similar to how confession—or "Sharing"—was performed in the Oxford Group: before Christ and another Christian. It is Christ who forgives, but it is the other Christian, a fellow human being, who provides concrete demonstration of that forgiveness:

> "Why shouldn't I go straight to God if I want to confess my sins? Why should I bother about another person interfering? The right and only person for my confession is God." Some people, when Sharing is explained to them, say this, and often with indignation. It is a nat-ural point of view to many, but it would be perhaps unchristian of us to ask them if they do confess to God and how much they confess and how much they keep back. We can, however, tell them that we do not deny that they can go straight to God if they wish and God will forgive them, but that if they wish for a sure and certain knowl-edge that their past sins—and all of them—are to be wiped out, once and for all, these sins must be brought into the open and honestly faced. To put them into words, before Christ and another Christian, as a witness, is the only healthy way of making sure that the spiri-tual system is virtually cleansed. (*What Is the Oxford Group?* 32)

Herein lies the possibility for spiritual growth. Through confession to another human being and God, to what Bakhtin calls the transgredient self or "over-I," the alcoholic can move beyond shame and fear. As Jung wrote, "we are all in some way kept asunder by our secrets" (*Modern Man in Source of a Soul* 36), and it "is only with the help of confession that I am able to throw myself into the arms of humanity freed at last from the burden of moral exile" (35). For Bakhtin also, confession is a means of bodily affirming values—hence, acting ethically—and taking respon-sibility for our place in the world.

Bakhtin also writes of the possibility for spiritual growth for those who listen to the confession. Even though the confession is an act rather than art, the audience could aestheticize it. The audience could consummate speakers, view them as heroes, sum up their lives, judge them or critique the telling of their stories. If the confession is aestheticized, it usually oc-curs after meetings and is typically minimalized. The more typical role of the audience at AA meetings is what Bakhtin calls edification:

> In actualizing the edificatory purpose of confessional self-account-ing, I project myself into the *subiectum* and reproduce within my-self the *subiectum*'s inner event, but I do so for purposes of my own spiritual growth, my own enrichment through accumulated spiritual experience. Confessional self-accounting informs and teaches about

God, for, as we see, by way of solitary self-accounting one gains cognizance of God and becomes aware of the faith that is already living within life itself (life-as-lived-faith). ("Author and Hero" 149)

To benefit from the act of another's confession, the audience "must neither reproduce this act (imitatively) nor contemplate it artistically" but "react to it with an answering act" (148). Bakhtin continues:

> I stand over against the *subiectum* of a confessional self-accounting in the unitary and unique event of being that encompasses *both* of us, and my answering act must not isolate him in that event; the yet-to-be future of the event conjoins both of us and determines our mutual relationship (both of us stand over against one another in God's world). (149)

One of the most frequent comments made about speakers by newcomers is something like "I felt like the speaker was telling my story." One of the bodily ways that this idea is conveyed, both to the speaker and to the listeners, is the nodding of heads as the speaker confesses what the audience has also lived. In this sense, the audience participates in the speaker's confession as if it were their own.

It is important to see the confessional moments in AA talks as part of a process. It is not the act of confession that is of utmost importance but the act of confession within the context of the acts of a new life, which includes service to others, that brings about change. Anne S., wife of Dr. Bob, was fond of quoting James 2:17: "Even so faith, if it hath not works, is dead, being alone." Carl Jung, perhaps as a loose paraphrase of James, voiced a similar concern about the confessions that occur between patient and psychiatrist. Confession without a change in habits is also dead:

> It is obviously not enough for him [the patient] to know how and why he fell ill, for to understand the causes of an evil does very little towards curing it. We must never forget that the crooked paths of a neurosis lead to as many obstinate habits, and that, despite any amount of understanding, these do not disappear until they are replaced by other habits. But habits are only won by exercise, and appropriate education is the sole means to this end. The patient must be, as it were, prodded into other paths, and this always requires an educating will. (*Modern Man in Search of a Soul* 45)

Bill W. acknowledged this theme of Jung's theory by referring to him as a man "great in spirit and action." Since the early days of AA, newcomers were of necessity quickly moved from confession and understanding into action. Bill W. described the process: "You'd take a guy into a hospital and he'd go in there. He'd come out jittery, and you'd take him to visit another guy. Then he was a full blown sponsor" (AA Talk).

12

Autobiography: Moving from Isolation and Finding Boundaries

> To see and comprehend the author of a work means to see and comprehend another, alien consciousness and its world, that is, another subject ("Du"). With *explanation* there is only one consciousness, one subject; with *comprehension* there are two consciousnesses and two subjects. There can be no dialogic relationship with an object, and therefore explanation has no dialogic aspects (except formal, rhetorical ones). Understanding is always dialogic to some degree.
> —M. M. Bakhtin, "The Problem of the Text"

While the moments of confessional self-accounting within a story are not transformative in themselves, they are preparatory. Speakers have consciously identified themselves, before God and other alcoholics, with actions that they once hid in shame. During these moments, speakers lose awareness of the audience and speak the confession to themselves, in what might even appear (at times) to be a trancelike, spiritual state. They say words so that *they* can hear them. But the audience is there nonetheless. When speakers regain a sense of the audience, they have learned—at that moment, as they reflect on the confession, or through repetitive retellings—that the contents of their confessions have lost power over them. They have spoken of their worst horrors against others, and their audience reacted with nods. There are no forces of social control. There is no blame, censure, or punishment.

With their nods, the audience has communed with the speaker, but the speaker is now in a moment of isolation. As alcoholics with alcoholic pasts, the speakers have needed to separate themselves from others to move past their relationship to self—their guilt, shame, and remorse. This move is supported by the middle steps (Steps Four through Nine), which ask alcoholics to deal with their pasts. These steps and the moments of confessional self-accounting release speakers from past behavior. A new identity and new behavior can begin, but not in this moment of isolation. Speakers must now commune with their audience. This happens in moments of autobiography, which frame the confessional self-accounting. And, as speakers tell their stories over and over, many of the confessional moments also become more like autobiography. The events that were confessed enter narrative time and are now shared with the audience. The stories of old-timers are more fully autobiographical, though certainly not like print autobiographies. What the old-timers have learned is to place their voices among other voices, to move from speaking *before* others to speaking *with* others.

For Bakhtin, autobiography is a form of self-objectification, but speakers do not speak to themselves: "Neither in biography or autobiography does the *I-for-myself* (my relationship to myself) represent the organizing, constitutive moment of form" ("Author and Hero" 151). This self-objectification began with confession, where important biographical events are first voiced, if not narrated. The self becomes further objectified with autobiography, but the author and hero are not fused. Rather, the author and hero are coeval and can, in effect, change rhetorical places. The author identifies with and speaks for the hero (as the author says, this hero is who I am), but the hero also speaks for the author as the audience associates the consummated hero (although, I should add, the hero of autobiography is not fully consummated, not as finished and complete as the heroes of fiction) with the unconsummated author. We can see, even at this preliminary juncture, that we have moved into a form of discourse that is both transformative and normative. Constructing the hero as a recovering alcoholic, in Michael K.'s words, is a promise to act differently:

> Once the *community* knew me as a man not responsible for the past, but obligated to future responsibility, *I* knew myself in the same way. And knowing, I am discovering, has much to do with both departing from the past and moving toward the future, with both being and becoming, with healing. (163)

While we might be more complicated and more unpredictable than the heroes we create, they do constitute an identity that we can move away from or toward.

This is how we might expect Bakhtin to explain the transformative effects of autobiography: Authors create heroes to whom they must answer. Bakhtin adds, however, that autobiography can also be an act of communion. As authors assume the role of narrator (a persona, an identity) in order to tell a story and create a hero, they become possessed by an "Other." What Bakhtin means is that as they assume the role of a narrator within a particular culture they take on a social role that carries with it established ways of behaving and thinking. He writes:

> The other who possesses me does not come into conflict with my *I-for-myself,* so long as I do not sever myself axiologically from the world of others, so long as I perceive myself within a collective (a family, a nation, civilized mankind). In this case, the axiological position of the other within me is *authoritative* for me; he can narrate the story of my life and I shall be in full inner agreement with him. So long as my life proceeds in indissoluble unity with the collective of others, it is interpreted, constructed, and organized (with respect to all the constituents it shares with the world of others) on the plane of another's possible consciousness of my life; my life is perceived and constructed as a possible story that might be told about it by the other to still others (to descendants). My consciousness of a possible narrator, the axiological context of a possible narrator, organizes my acts, thoughts, and feelings where, with respect to their value, they are involved in the world of others. Each one of these constituents of my life may be perceived within the whole of a narrative—a narrative that is the story of my life, each one may be found on everyone's lips. My contemplation of my own life is no more than the anticipation of others' recollections about my life—of recollections by descendants or simply by family members and close relatives (the amplitude of any life's biographicalness may be variable); the values that organizes life itself as well as the recollection of life are one and the same. ("Author and Hero" 153)

To speak about one's story within the culture of an AA meeting is to live the tradition and culture of the organization. The speaker uses the values of that community to interpret his or her life and construct the heroes to whom he or she will answer. As the story of a speaker's life is "found on everyone's lips," the speaker performs an act of communion. As the speaker learns to speak as the others in that community speak, he or she shares a new identity. In Bakhtin's words:

> The hero and the narrator can easily change places in this case: whether it is I who tell of another, of someone close to me (someone with whom I live one and the same axiological life in a family, in a nation, in mankind, in the world), or whether it is the other who tells of me, in either case I am still woven into the narrative in the same tones and in the same form as he is. Without detaching myself from the life in which *others* are the heroes and the world is *their* surrounding world, I—as narrator of this life—become assimilated, as it were, to its heroes. When I narrate my own life, in which the heroes are those who are others for me, I am step by step woven into its formal structure (I participate in my own life, but I am not the hero of it); I put myself in the hero's place, I captivate myself through my own narration. Wherever I am in solidarity with others, the forms

in which others are axiologically perceived are transposed upon myself. It is thus that the narrator becomes the hero. (154)

Members of AA frequently acknowledged that they rely on each other to stay sober. It is within the community of other alcoholics that they assume new values and new identities. As they speak, sharing the stories of their lives, constructing heroes, they do so by taking on the values of the community. Each time they speak, they reinforce those values. So they construct heroes that are like the other heroes of the community. In short, the genre of AA storytelling—if it could be so called—not only embodies the values and norms of that social setting (a role for speaker and audience and a ritual through which they commune), the telling also enacts that culture. Speakers come to know themselves and others as they speak.

The autobiography of published memoirs is quite different. Pete Hamill's *A Drinking Life* can serve as an example of polished autobiography in print (Hamill is a journalist and novelist), written by a man who sobered up without AA. Hamill tells the story—his story—of growing up in an alcoholic family (his father was an alcoholic, as were many of his relatives) within an alcoholic culture (many of his neighbors in various Irish-Catholic sections of Brooklyn were also heavy drinkers) and an alcoholic period of American history (following the repeal of prohibition). Yet, the reader might be struck by how often alcohol is in the background as a form of narrative noise. Hamill does not only tell the story of his drinking, as Caroline Knapp does in *Drinking;* he tells the story of a boy who grows into a man in a fullness that is never found in AA narratives. He tells of school yard fights, early sexual experiences, searching for a career, and other events that do not directly relate to alcoholism. Consider, for example, the following passages about "Betty the Whore," who lived near the Hamill family as World War II was culminating:

> Up Twelfth Street, in one of the buildings across from the Factory, there was a woman with flaming red hair who was called Betty the Whore (we pronounced the word *who*-uh). We would see her in the late afternoons, coming down the street in very high heels, short shirt, and jacket with padded shoulders. She changed her hairstyle all the time, letting it flow out, piling it on top of her head, flattening it under a pillbox hat. She was also the first woman in the neighborhood to wear slacks, which caused people to stare at her just as much as the tangerine hair. Most afternoons, when she started her walk, men would slowly step out of the bars, just to look at her, and they'd yell at her and she'd yell back and then she'd get on a trolley car and go off toward Flatbush Avenue. The men would all laugh and nudge each other and then go back into the bars. (48)

If this passage were compared to the kind of autobiography in AA narratives, one would recognize that Hamill has contextualized and aestheticized his narrative. He attentively sets the character in a particular historical and cultural period with the pronunciation of "*who*-uh," the novelty of her wearing slacks, her pillbox hat. Hamill also consummates this character. A few pages later, he adds a short chapter to finish her story:

> That winter, Betty the Whore's husband came home. He was a gaunt, hollow-eyed man who had been a German prisoner for two years. But when he went into the building there were no Welcome Home signs and no Betty either. We all heard about the way he reacted. He went into Unbeatable Joe's and got very drunk. Then he started throwing glasses and ashtrays and punched out the mirror in the men's room. The other men were very gentle. They took him home and put him to bed.
>
> The next day, he left the Neighborhood and never came back. (63)

Hamill tells his story and the story of those around him, and he tells it in a way that allows the reader to experience a man explaining his life as if reading about characters in a novel. We find no moments of confessional self-accounting. And we find few moments of self-reflection, a grappling to find a sense of self. We can only imagine what happened before the story is put to paper, when Hamill was in the process of changing. Hamill, the hero of the autobiography, seems finished, and Hamill, the author, seems to know who this hero is. He constructs his hero, in Bakhtin's words, through a *surplus* of vision. In other words, he knows things about the hero that even the hero cannot know about himself; he has the knowledge to complete the hero's life.

In Hamill's autobiography, heroes are consummated or killed off, which raises ethical questions for both Bakhtin and Kenneth Burke. In *A Rhetoric of Motives,* Burke begins with an analysis of suicide and murder and moves to a discussion of war and communion; throughout this move, he writes of identity and transformation. We kill off others (similar to Bakhtin's consummation of heroes), Burke says, to mark their identities and form our own identity, for "the so-called 'desire to kill' a certain person is much more properly analyzable as a desire to *transform the principle* which that person *represents*" (13). We hope that killing off others—including the former self—can bring lasting change. But Burke sees death, real or textual, as the moment at which identity is fixed *and* the moment at which transformation begins:

> [T]he imagery of slaying is a special case of transformation, and transformation involves the ideas and imagery of *identification*. That is: the *killing* of something is the *changing* of it, and the statement of the thing's nature before and after the change is an *identifying* of it. (20)

It is the aim of AA stories to ritually transform the drinking self while maintaining an identity with it. For Bakhtin, this means creating a hero who then creates the author.[1]

An AA speaker assumes the persona of a recovering alcoholic and so interprets his or her life through the values of the community of AA, tells of his or her former self repeatedly, not to kill off the former self and complete the transformation into a new identity, but to come to know the former self and then keep that self alive.[2] The new identity of the re-covering alcoholic, thus, depends upon a ritualized and repetitive reiden-tification with the former self (the practicing alcoholic) and the realiza-tion, also borne through constant repetition, that the former self could become the future self.[3] Every telling of one's story involves a number of acts of identity. The speaker reaffirms an identity with his or her former self (I am the person who did these things, the person who takes respon-sibility for these things) even as he or she creates (with each retelling) an increasing sense of distance from that self. One may, during the moments of confession, bring yet another aspect of one's ego, one's sense of shame or remorse about past events, before God and an audience so that it has less power over him or her. The speaker reaffirms his or her present per-sona, his or her identity as a recovering alcoholic, which entails member-ship within a community, which is an identification with a future self, the self that the speaker promises to become. Finally, the speaker identifies with those around him or her, other members of AA in the room and those outside the room, those who have played some role in the speaker's life.

The practice of keeping the former self alive is AA's means to trans-formation; its practice of allowing others to live—and speak for them-selves—is its ethic. These others constitute what Bakhtin considers to be the second class of heroes in autobiography, the dramatis personæ:

> The representation of them includes many transgredient features; they may function not only as *characters,* but even as *types* (the fea-tures transgredient to them are given in the consciousness of the main hero—the narrator, who is the biographical hero proper, thus mov-ing him closer to the author's position). Their life may often have a finished *fabula,* as long as the latter is not too intimately intertwined with the life of the biographical hero—the narrator. ("Author and Hero" 162)

When Bakhtin calls the dramatis personæ *characters* or *types,* he means that they are consummated within the narrative. They are finished—their story is a *fabula* with a beginning, middle, and end—and they are there to serve the narrator as the narrator tells his or her story. The narrator is within time and changing; the dramatic personæ are beyond time and fixed. They are also "given in the consciousness of the main hero," that is, the audience knows them only through the narrator. While narrators might not possess an excess of vision about their own selves (and so have difficulty fully consummating their hero, the author's identity within the text), they might feel that they have a *surplus* or excess of vision about others. They might think that they can consummate these others, tell their entire stories (as Hamill told the story of Betty the Whore) in a neat *fabula*. The more ethical approach, Bakhtin believes, is to treat the dramatis personæ of one's autobiography as if they had the freedom to act in ways that we would not expect them to act or, to put it differently, as if we could not fully know them or predict how they will act or change.[4]

Consummating the dramatis personæ, killing them off with a neat *fabula*, reducing them to characters or types, does not frequently occur in AA stories. In autobiography, the dramatis personæ, as extensions of the narrator, serving the author's purpose to construct his or her hero, are typically exteriors, flat surfaces, virtually reduced to stage props. The author uses them to justify his or her hero's actions or stage the hero's transformation. In AA stories, we find a different ethos, as created by working the steps and taking on the persona of an old-timer. Speakers accept responsibility for their actions, as does Dr. Bob in his last talk:

> I just don't want to bump myself off with the pleasures of alcohol. So I'm not going to do it. I'm never going to do it, as long as I do the things I am supposed to do. I know what those things are. If I should ever get tight, I certainly would never have anyone to blame for it. (AA Talk)

In a discourse that says the individual is not important, within an ethos that demands personal responsibility, the dramatis personæ are allowed to live; they are recognized as being more complicated than the narrator-hero's vision of them.[5] In *Toward a Philosophy of the Act,* Bakhtin describes this as love:

> The valued manifoldness of Being as human (as correlated with the human being) can present itself only to a loving contemplation. Only love is capable of holding and making fast all this multiformity and diversity, without losing and dissipating it, without leaving behind a mere skeleton of basic lines and sense-moments. Only un-self-interested love on the principle of "I love him not because he is good, but he is good because I love him," only lovingly interested attention, is capable of generating a sufficiently intent power to encompass and retain the concrete manifoldness of Being, without impoverishing and schematizing it. An indifferent or hostile reaction is always a reaction that impoverishes and decomposes its object: it seeks to pass over the object in all its manifoldness, to ignore it or to overcome it. The very function of indifference biologically consists in freeing us from the manifoldness of Being, diverting us from what is inessential for us practically—a kind of economy or preservation from being dissipated in the manifoldness. And this is the function of forgetting as well. (64)

Bakhtin is, in a rather complicated and philosophical work, arguing for the ethics of allowing others (the dramatis personæ) to speak and live (to have their manifoldness of Being). Love and memory allow us "to slow down and *linger intently* over an object" (64). Indeed, this is an effect of telling one's story: The speaker begins to accept personal responsibility, to establish boundaries between self and others (as the speaker tells his or her story but not the stories of others), and to strive to understand others (to see others as an interior, accept their uniqueness, rather than reduce them to characters or types). Paradoxically, it is through establishing boundaries with dramatis personæ that AA speakers begin to commune with others. After all, people who do not have clear boundaries between self and others can only relate to themselves or their own projections.

The process of establishing boundaries between self and others, thus, is central to the entire program and the creation of a new identity. As speakers learn to tell *their* stories—and not someone else's—they learn to see themselves as separate and apart from these dramatis personæ. Speakers come to know that they have no control over the actions of other people or random events and so begin to envision a self that is a part of some social context and yet also apart from it. Bill W. describes his own development in this respect in a June 27, 1940, letter to Larry J.:

> At first I used to make a personal issue of every case. I tried to carry everyone on my back which was, of course, damned near broke on many occasions. For six long months I labored in the vineyard with rising and falling hopes, having to admit at the end of that time that not a soul had surely laid hold of the Master, not excepting myself. As an alcoholic I am rated as an easy going temperament yet these failures, my feeling of economic insecurity, and rather poor health, conspired to throw me sometimes into spasms of real hysterics, when I tore my hair and lay on the bed and beat it. This brought me to the good healthy realization that there were plenty of situations still left in the world over which I had no personal power—that if I was so ready to admit that to be the case with alcohol so I must make the same admission with respect to everything else. I would have to be still and Know that The Great Physician stood by holding out his hand which I might grasp. Such has been my schooling in the principles of humility and spiritual dependence.

Bill went on to recount how a man had "committed suicide in my house mainly because I kept on making it easy for him to keep doing as he pleased." In the letter, Bill describes moving from acknowledging that he is powerless over alcohol to acknowledging that he is powerless over other people and events. The identity of alcoholics, which became so clouded and enmeshed with the actions of others during their drinking days, finds some sense of clarity as they tell their stories and allows others to tell theirs. And so, in many ways, the stories told in AA do not achieve the fullness of autobiography or fiction; heroes remain unconsummated, and the stories of those around the hero remain unfinished or even substantially untold.

A Drinking Life, an autobiography, would read as a novel if not for one thing: Hamill is writing about himself, and so the reader wonders what about his life has been left out and why. When Hamill writes about a handful or so of early sexual experiences, the reader might wonder: Has he described all these experiences? Why did he describe these and not some other? When he writes, for example, about living with Shirley Mac-Laine, the reader might wonder why he writes about this relationship in broad strokes. Autobiography is, Bakhtin believes, an unstable genre because we know the author's life is fuller than the life of the hero captured on the page, even when the author makes an honest attempt to tell all. The reader senses a fullness that collapses moment to moment. The heroes of autobiography are not as consummated as the heroes of fiction, and the heroes of AA storytelling are even less finished than those of autobiography.

How, then, does Hamill's text differ from the autobiographical moments of AA narratives? In AA storytelling, working within an oral tradition, there is little—sometimes *no*—time devoted to contextualization. Events that do not relate to one's history of drinking are excluded (the listeners know they are hearing a fragment and, thus, that the hero is not consummated); others are not discussed as characters but as people whom the speaker has harmed or people whom the speaker has come to understand more fully. Perhaps, more importantly, a frequent character in AA narratives is missing from Hamill's narration: the character of alcoholism as a disease. In AA narratives, alcoholism is a character that acts upon and eventually consumes the speaker. In Hamill's narrative, he describes the acts of drinking and the acts that come from his drinking. Early in the narrative these acts are a theme, but not always the focus. Toward the end of the narrative, the act and acts of drinking start to dominate the story, but alcoholism is never seen as an agent acting upon Hamill.

I will have more to say about the autobiographical moments of AA stories in the next chapter, when I discuss chronotopes. Here is a brief summary. The talks of AA members usually begin with a brief description of the speaker's childhood or life before drinking. This portion of the talk emphasizes the uniqueness of the speaker. He or she might have had a horrible childhood or a good childhood. He or she might have grown up in the Midwest or the South. This portion is rather brief, more suggestive than anything like a full narrative. Often the speaker comments on how, even when growing up in a normal family, he or she felt different. The next section, though events are not always told in chronological order, deals with the first drink and early drinking experiences. The speaker often comments on how the first drink made him or her feel normal. As his or her disease progresses, the speaker's story emphasizes similarity: It becomes the story of all alcoholics. Then the speaker tells of coming to AA, struggling with sobriety and achieving a new identity and a better life. While these events might seem to form an autobiography, I have called them autobiographical moments because they are really a string of loosely connected anecdotes rather than a full narrative. The gaps are glaring and crucial.

13

Chronotopes: The Order Behind Fragments of a Life

> The chronotope is the place where the knots of narrative are tied and untied. It can be said without qualification that to them belongs the meaning that shapes narrative.
>
> —M. M. Bakhtin,
> "Forms of Time and Chronotope in the Novel"

With his concept of chronotope, Bakhtin wanted to move past the simplistic notion that context is simply transcribed into text. Morson and Emerson explain: "In its primary sense, a chronotope is a way of understanding experience; it is a specific form-shaping ideology for understanding the nature of events and actions" (367). To understand a genre, Bakhtin argues, we must understand its chronotope. He writes: "The chronotope in literature as an intrinsic *generic* significance. It can even be said that it is precisely the chronotope that defines genre and genre distinctions, for in literature the primary category in the chronotope is time" ("Forms of Time" 84–85).

While Bakhtin speaks of a chronotope as dealing with a particular way of conceptualizing time and space, he fairly consistently uses five categories to describe each chronotope: time, plot, the hero, the world, and history. For example, the Novel of Ordeal, in which the hero faces a series of difficulties that test his or her character, evolved from the Greek romance ("The *Bildungsroman*" 12), through early Christian hagiographies and medieval chivalric tales to the baroque novel (13). As he historically traces this genre, Bakhtin shows that a chronotope is not some timeless or decontextualized cognitive structure; rather, it originates at a historical moment *and* develops through history within the tradition of a genre. Time, in the Novel of Ordeal, for example, is "characterized by a violation of temporal categories" (15); it is "psychologically colored," either expanded or condensed, as the temporal is reduced to "a series of tests" (11, 15). The plot presents "deviations from the normal course of the hero's life" (14). In other words, it does not present the major events of one's life (birth, schooling, marriage, job, children, etc.) in chronological order, as in biographies. Rather, it presents "events that essentially should *not* take place, that only separate two contiguous moments of the biography from one another, that retard the course of normal life, but do not change it" (14). Given this approach to plot, we should not be surprised that the hero is "complete and unchanging" (12). The hero "does not alter the social face of the world, nor does he restructure it, and he does not claim to" (16). The world created for this genre is a "mere background for the hero" (15); it "lacks independence and historicity" (15). The only aspect of actual world that enters the text is found in the "ideological content of the idea" that is tested (13), which might be considered its dominant feature. The entire point of this kind of novel is to assert the cultural importance of some quality or idea, say bravery. Thus, the hero remains unchangingly brave, despite the seemingly unending series of harrowing experiences he or she must face.

In autobiography, the genre closest to the stories told at AA meetings, a hero emerges that is not yet as distinct as the heroes found in works of fiction. While the hero might be more clearly defined than the hero in the Novels of Ordeal or the Travel Novel, perhaps even undergoing a spiritual crisis and rebirth, "the hero himself remains essentially unchanged" (17). This might surprise readers of autobiography, who feel that the hero often undergoes a radical change, even to the degree that we can speak of a "before self" and an "after self." Perhaps, what Bakhtin means is that the hero of autobiography only changes to become more like the persona of the narrative voice. In this sense, at least, the hero does not really change.

In this genre, Bakhtin says, the hero and the author can change places. This is not simply a result of the material fact that the author and the hero of autobiography share the same body; rather, it is because "the hero is incapable of being consummated within the bounds of biographical value" ("Author and Hero" 166). The "biographical utterance" is "always enveloped by a naive faith" (165). In other words, the author (and readers as well) believes that the author is the hero. It is this "naive faith" or "biographical value" that preempts the consummation of the hero. For the hero to be consummated the author would need to assume the role of a "pure *artist*" and shape the hero from outside rather than speak of his or her interior life. The artist, Bakhtin argues, works from a "fundamental and essential excess of seeing" (166). The artist, in other words, knows everything about the hero—even what happens before and after the story proper, even what happens in the gaps of the narration. In fiction, the author creates the hero and the hero's world. The author of autobiography, a genre constructed upon "naive faith," is attempting to relate a life, told in "realistic," "biographical time" ("The *Bildungsroman*" 17), that is being lived within a world, linked "with historical time and with epoch" (18), that cannot be comprehensively *seen*. While we might assume that an author can speak with greatest authority about his or her own life, Bakhtin feels that there are significant limits to self-knowledge:

> If the world of others is axiologically authoritative for me, then it assimilates me-as-the-other to itself (it does so, of course, in those respects in which it is authoritative for me). I come to know a considerable portion of my own biography from what is said by others, by people close to me, as well as in the emotional tonality of these others; my birth and my descent, the events of family life and national life in my early childhood (that is, everything that could not have been understood or simply could not even have been perceived by a child). All these moments are indispensable for reconstructing an even minimally intelligible and coherent picture of my life and its world; I—as narrator of my own life—come to know all of them from the lips of others who are its heroes. ("Author and Hero" 154)

In autobiography, we have an unfinished hero and an unstable—ultimately, an unknowable—world; even the "boundary between the horizon and the surrounding world or environment is unstable" (166). There is no "excess of seeing," because the author cannot possess a complete knowledge of self or know everything about others. Thus, the very form of autobiography is unstable as well; it never achieves a completeness of plot.

The structure of the stories told in AA comes from the autobiographical moments, a rather unstable genre from its beginnings. In early autobiography (classical biographies or autobiographies and early Christian confessions), the genre was frequently intermixed with confessional self-accounting.[1] Even in modern forms of autobiography, a "confessional tone often irrupts into the biographical self-containedness of a life" (150), the recounting of the events of a typical life—birth, schooling, marriage, children, job, etc.—that dominate the plot of autobiography. While autobiographies, especially those written for publication as opposed to private diaries, have a sense of structure in that they are told in chronological order, the narrator often seems incapable of providing summarizing transitions between the segments of the author's life that are narrated and the gaps that represent what was not remembered or what was withheld or deemed unimportant. While the author might write an autobiography in "naive faith," a modern audience often read like critics, wondering, "What really happened?" Or "What is the author hiding?"[2]

Autobiographies written for publication (which, within current publishing practices, means written for money, maybe even "told to" a professional writer) attempt to convey a narrative fullness that they never quite achieve, but the stories told at AA meetings even fall short of the unstable genre of autobiography. Indeed, the speaker often struggles in a formless meandering, expressing uncertainty about how to begin or proceed. Interlaced within the stories are comments like these:

> "I don't know where to start. Maybe I will just begin at the beginning."
> "I guess I am just rambling now."
> "Oh, I was going to say something about . . ."

The speaker may repeatedly lapse into silence, jumble the chronology, and seem lost, incapable of constructing a narrative. The stories seem spontaneous; what is told and how it is told surprises even the speaker. I have heard only one speaker read from prepared notes, and even he occasionally looked up to elaborate on certain points and soon found himself lost, unable to remember if he had just finished point eight or point nine.

Some stories are told in a stricter chronological order and possess a cleaner narrative line, usually the stories in print (those in the Big Book or in commercially published autobiographies like Knapp's *Drinking: A Love Story*) or the stories told by old-timers. But even these stories do not really conclude; they simply trail off as speakers begin to talk about what AA has done for them. The speakers do not possess a "surplus of seeing" about their own stories; they have not consummated themselves.[3] There are gaps, and the speaker seems quite unable to fill them. And so the hero remains unconsummated, beyond the seeing of the author.

In the stories told at meetings, there is a sense of chronology, maybe provided more by the audience than the speaker, in that the narrated events did occur within what Bakhtin calls "biographical time": time marked as the hero "passes through unrepeatable, individual stages" ("The *Bildungsroman*" 22). The hero might, for example, move through one of several series: guilt —> retribution —> redemption; guilt —> punishment —> redemption —> purification —> blessedness; or sinful life —> crisis —> redemption —> sainthood ("Forms of Time" 128–29). For most AA narratives, the stages are remarkably similar: speakers describe their childhoods as a time when they felt "different"; speakers begin drinking, life seems wonderful, things fall apart, the disease progresses; speakers find AA, struggle with early sobriety, and eventually find a better life. But the events are not always told in order; it is not always clear when something happened, and speakers may even express confusion about when this or that happened. This portion of the story is also further fragmented by its anecdotal structure. It is not one story, a series of events brought together with transitions, but a string of anecdotes that the speaker moves in and out of without transition.

The clearest distinction, however, between autobiography and AA stories is that the hero changes, or, said in Bakhtin's terminology, the drunkolog and the "now" segments of the story reflect different chronotopes and present different heroes. Bakhtin writes:

> Chronotopes are mutually inclusive, they co-exist, they may be interwoven with, replace or oppose one another, contradict one another or find themselves in ever more complex interrelationships. The relationships themselves that exist *among* chronotopes cannot enter into any of the relationships contained *within* chronotopes. The general characteristic of these interactions is that they are *dialogical* (in the broadest sense of the word). ("Forms of Time" 252)

It is, thus, the shift in chronotopes between the drunkolog and the "now" sections that rhetorically mark a transformation.

The chronotope of the drunkolog reflects speakers' attempts to understand the events of their drinking days as the process of a disease. It is clear, if we compare the talks of newcomers and old-timers, that speakers grow into an understanding of this chronotope as they work the program and repeatedly tell their stories:

- Throughout the drunkolog, narrators speak from a place beyond the hero. In the talks of newcomers the sense of dissonance may be slight. In the talks of old-timers, the dissonance is profound. And so the narration is always layered and double voiced. Speakers, as recovering alcoholics and as members of AA, speak the words they once spoke as a practicing alcoholic.
- The events that mark biographical time (childhood, schooling, marriage, children, etc.) become less significant; the passage of time is marked by anecdotes that, even when told out of chronological order, plot the progression of the disease of alcoholism.
- Events are narrated as if they could occur in practically any historical era or location. This serves to facilitate the sense of identity among alcoholics and emphasize the overpowering effect of alcohol on the hero.
- The progression of the disease is accretive. The former self of the speaker becomes more disordered and delusional, often gradually, maybe even without reaching a crisis point, though the former self does realize at some point that he or she can no longer deny the effects of the disease—but these moments of clarity are also moments of utter despair.[4]
- The progression of the disease is viewed as a necessity. Every speaker experiences the same progression of the disease that is beyond the control of the former self. Particular decisions and actions, whether good or bad, have no effect on the course of the disease.

- As the disease (considered an exterior force) controls the alcoholic more thoroughly, the alcoholic loses the ability to control even mundane events of day-to-day life.[5]
- Identity is gradually lost as the alcoholic loses contact with family and friends, now living almost exclusively among other practicing alcoholics. The alcoholic is on the fringe of ordinary life.

As newcomers tell their stories, they tend to feel a great deal of guilt and shame for the actions described in the drunkolog, for they have not yet learned how to place the events of their lives within the chronotope. They tend to associate their actions with some defect of character. As they listen to the stories of old-timers, they begin to view their actions as necessary effects of the progression of the disease. As long as they continued to drink, things could not be otherwise. The effect of this chronotope, its consuming sense of necessity, establishes a strong identity between speaker and audience (they come to see that every alcoholic's story is essentially the same) as it allows the speaker to move past guilt and shame (they come to see that the disease was in control). The hero of this section might seem consummated (a position from which the speaker attempts to find distance), but his or her "story" is narrated as unfinished (the speaker acknowledges that he or she can, once again, become a practicing alcoholic).

As speakers come to the end of their drunkologs, as they begin to speak of their lives "now," as members of AA, as nondrinking alcoholics, we find a new narrative time, a time in which "individual emergence is inseparably linked to historical emergence" ("The *Bildungsroman*" 23) and a different chronotope that is dialogically opposed to the drunkolog chronotope. This chronotope is similar to that found in the works of Rabelais and Goethe. Bakhtin explains:

> It is no longer man's own private affair. He emerges *along with the world* and he reflects the historical emergence of the world itself. He is no longer within an epoch, but on the border between two epochs, at the transition point from one to the other. This transition is accomplished in him and through him. He is forced to become a new, unprecedented type of human being. What is happening here is precisely the emergence of a new man. The organizing force held by the future is therefore extremely great here—and this is not, of course, the private biographical future, but the historical future. It is as though the very *foundations* of the world are changing, and man must change along with them. (23–24)

In AA narratives, it is not so much that the individual emerges or that the world emerges; it is that the recovering alcoholic finds a new life within the organization of AA as that organization functions within and against a broader culture. Nonetheless, the shift in narrative time is the same—a shift toward the potential and the future. The chronotope of the "now" segment of the story has the following characteristics:

- The hero is reborn into ordinary life (O'Reilly, *Sobering Tales* 120). Anecdotes might recount returning to work, reestablishing relationships with family and friends, and so on.
- The hero is described as progressively improving through working the steps and becoming more involved in the program. The hero moves past fear, shame, and resentment to serenity and acceptance. No specific, historical person is described as the ideal toward which the hero moves, although other members of AA might be mentioned as having provided some key insight or support. This personal improvement is seen as being a result of working the program.
- Events are perceived as being part of God's plan. The necessity of the disease of alcoholism is replaced by the order of God's plan. There are no accidents. The hero experiences specific problems because he or she needs to learn a particular lesson, and all difficulties are viewed as an opportunity to improve and grow as a spiritual person. God does not allow more problems than the hero can handle, and God provides the resources and support that the hero needs to solve the problems. In contrast to this belief in God's plan is the belief that "bad things just happen" and need to be accepted. What allows these two apparently contradictory views to coexist is the overarching belief that the hero has little or no control over many—though certainly not all— life events.
- Speakers achieve transcendence. They learn that happiness and serenity are products of the way that they think, which they can control, rather than a necessary effect of the events of their lives, over which they often have little control. Speakers recount their continuing struggles, but the focus is on a vastly improved quality of life. They look to the future and the promise of an even more satisfying life.
- Identity is regained or discovered.

The "now" chronotope, it should be noted, is not always present or fully developed. Those early in recovery may gloss over this segment of their talks, for they have not even come to an understanding of the chronotope of the drunkolog. Those who are further in recovery tend to have a clear understanding of the chronotope of the drunkolog, but they present an idealized and artificial version of the "now" segment, for they are creating the hero that they wish to become, a hero and a way of seeing the world that they do not yet fully understand. Old-timers are more likely to embody, in content and voice, the chronotope of the "now" section even while they blur the boundaries between the former self and the present self. They are more likely to discuss their current struggles, including their move from "alcoholic thinking," which O'Reilly describes as a shift from "binary thinking to non-binary thinking" (*Sobering Tales* 121–26).

What is perhaps the most distinct feature of the "now" chronotope is the voice (Bakhtin calls it "the author-creator"), which, in the talks of old-timers, speaks the events of the drunkolog and even seems outside the hero of the "now" section. As Bakhtin has said, the author-creator—that is, the persona of the author that operates within the text, the voice that speaks the story—remains outside of the chronotope of the narration:

> [T]he author-creator, finding himself outside the chronotopes of the world he represents in his work, is nevertheless not simply outside but as it were tangential to these chronotopes. . . . Even had he created an autobiography or a confession of the most astonishing truthfulness, all the same he, as its creator, remains outside the world he has represented in his work. If I relate (or write about) an event that has just happened to me, then I as the *teller* (or writer) of this event am already outside the time and space in which the event occurred. ("Forms of Time" 256)

For newcomers, the voice of the author-creator—the voice of the person who bodily stands before others at a meeting—is that of an unfinished person who looks to the hero of the "now" portion of the story as the person he or she is in the process of becoming. The voice quivers and changes pitch, breaks to regain control, and weeps as the speaker tells of the miracle of a new life. For old-timers, the dynamic between the voice of the author-creator and the hero of the "now" portion of the story is inverted. The voice—now calm, rhythmic, even sermonic at times—is that of the program. As old-timers speak of their shortcomings, imperfections, and "dry drunks," some of which may have happened last week or yesterday, their voices seem above the turbulence of stress and worry. Thus, their voices—the voice of the program—reposition the events of their stories, whether they are from the distant or recent past, into the ethos of the program. The hero that the old-timer moves toward is not the hero who acts in the "now"; rather, the old-timer moves toward the hero embodied in his or her voice and so comes, with each retelling, closer to embodying the ethos of the program.

There is a sense of time in AA stories, actually several senses of time, but, in the most basic sense, AA stories are without plot.[6] There is no certainty about where the speaker will lead the audience or about what the hero (who remains unconsummated) must do. Hayden White, in his analysis of historical narratives, has argued that plot cannot exist without law and that law cannot exist without a clearly specified notion of a legal subject. When we have plot, White says, we have a moral. We have an individual (or group of individuals) who can be judged and held responsible. Where there is no plot, there is no moral. As the stories in AA trail off, they resist a moral (13–14).[7]

The stories are self-consciously told in fragments. The speaker does not claim to tell his or her entire life story, nor does the audience expect to hear it. Yet, both speaker and audience experience a sense of fullness within the community of AA. For those listeners who understand the chronotopes behind the fragments, there is a sense of order within the openness, and the story of one speaker finds a completion in the stories of others. Bakhtin explains:

> Without these stories told by others, my life would not only lack fullness and clarity in its content, but would also remain internally dispersed, divested of any value-related *biographical unity*. The *fragments* of my life as I experienced them from within myself ("fragments" from the standpoint of the biographical whole) are, after all, capable of gaining only the inner unity of my *I-for-myself* (the future unity of a task), or the unity of confessional self-accounting, and *not* the unity of biography. For only the yet-to-be-achieved unity of the *I-for-myself* is immanent to the life that is lived and experienced from within. The inner principle of unity is not suited to biographical narration; my *I-for-myself* is incapable of *narrating* anything. But the axiological position of the other, which is so indispensable for biography, is the position closest to me: I immediately become involved in it through the others who are the heroes of my life and *through the narrators of my life*. Thus, the hero of a life may become the narrator of it. ("Author and Hero" 154–55)

By the axiological position of biography, Bakhtin means the way that the life of the speaker and the hero and the audience intersect. It is the nature of autobiography and biography to be fragmentary, yet completeness is achieved with others.[8] Just as the author and the hero might trade places, the hero of one person's story might trade places with the hero of another person's story. In AA, it works this way. Speakers tell their stories in fragments, whether they stand before an audience at a speaker meeting or contribute to a topic meeting. They tell some fragments at one meeting and more fragments at another meeting. But they also listen to others tell their stories. As they listen, they nod, accepting some of the fragments they hear as their own. The fragments of others begin to fill the gaps of their stories. The shared story of the community moves toward completeness, but the individuals can only speak fragments.

Conclusion

Moving from Newcomer to Old-Timer

> The wealth and diversity of speech genres are boundless because the various possibilities of human activity are inexhaustible, and because each sphere of activity contains an entire repertoire of speech genres that differentiate and grow as the particular sphere develops and becomes more complex.
> —M. M. Bakhtin, "The Problem of Speech Genres"

Fully initiated members of AA often comment on how much they have changed by attending meetings, working the steps, and telling their stories. It is not uncommon to hear one say, "AA has saved my life." To outsiders, these claims might seem exaggerated. We are, after all, living in an age of mass media that is supported by advertising. We are used to hearing hyperbole or outright distortions; we know how to hear claims and take them down a few notches to find a grain of truth. But members of AA do not consider these statements inflated. They do feel that they have changed, and they truly believe that AA has preempted an early death. As I attended open meetings for over three years I saw newcomers enter the program with horribly shattered lives, barely able to speak at their first meetings, and I witnessed their progress toward what the program calls serenity. They did not so much regain what they had lost through years of drinking; they found something new—a sane life, a place within a community, an acceptance of life on its own terms. I also watched as some newcomers repeatedly relapsed and eventually died.

Throughout this book, I have alluded to the differences between newcomers and old-timers, differences in how they speak at meetings and how they tell their stories. Certainly, members go through a long process of learning how to tell one's story, but members also accept that speakers tell their stories as they need to tell them *at that point in their spiritual development.* There is no right or wrong way to tell one's story, but, as I have argued, members do not grow without changing how they speak, and they cannot really change how they speak without experiencing growth. They grow by adopting—at first, mimicking—new ways of speaking, and these new ways of speaking become who they are as they grow into the style and genre that they could once only poorly mimic. In this chapter, I will summarize this process of growth, the member's growing into a tradition of storytelling, by contrasting the typical story told by newcomers and that told by old-timers.

The Newcomer's Story

When newcomers say, "Hello, I'm ———. I'm an alcoholic," when they begin to tell their stories for the first time, they may already be overwhelmed by an array of intense, maybe even conflicting, emotions that they cannot label or control. They may feel, even at this moment, that they will not be able to get through it, stand before an audience, and spend thirty minutes or so telling their stories. How they tell their stories will certainly reflect their mental states. In the coming minutes, they will move through a range of emotions: anxiety about how they are being viewed, fear of voicing and thus memorializing a past they would rather forget, sadness and a vague sense of loss, guilt about everything but mostly about their failure to meet the expectations of loved ones, and embarrassment for their past actions. They may move through moments of numbness and even feel themselves slipping into a trancelike state. After they return to their seats, they might not even remember most of what they said. As a storyteller, they may feel like they can gain control over an event here or there, but not the entire story. They will speak in fragments.

Newcomers usually speak of drinking and little else. At this point, it is all they really know. They will probably say little or nothing about their childhoods. If they do, they may offer it as an explanation for why they began to drink, for they may not have yet learned to take responsibility for their actions. As they speak of drinking and where drinking led them, they may lapse into a number of confessional moments, and they will hear their voices but not really know that they are speaking, certainly not know that they are speaking before others. Even when they have more control over the fragments of their drinking days, they remain close to the events. A hero has not yet emerged to create some separation between the drinking days and the life in AA. They may even need to stop and cry, ramble a while, and try to find their places again. They will probably not be very aware of their audience, except on occasion. They might, for example, relate an event that they feel is sad and then realize that some of the old-timers have laughed. They will be shocked and wonder why the old-timers see humor in something that is so sad.

When they speak of coming to AA, they will speak of struggles: their struggles to stop drinking, their relapses, their struggles with learning to work the steps, their struggles to understand and accept how they have

The Newcomer's Story

Narrative Voice

- The voice moves through quick shifts of emotions: sadness, fear, guilt, embarrassment, anxiety, etc.
- The speaker sees little—or no—humor in his or her story.
- The story is more fragmented. The speaker does not seem to control the narrative; rather, the events of the narrative engulf the speaker.

Childhood	*Drunkolog*	*Coming to AA*	*Now*
• Life apart from drinking is seen as insignificant. Little is said about childhood events or family of origin.	• The narrative voice seems to be the voice of the hero of the drunkolog.	• The hero is portrayed as being in a constant state of struggle.	• The speaker may express gratitude for a new life in AA, while the tenor of his or her voice conveys turmoil or conflict.
• If family of origin is mentioned, it may be viewed as a cause of drinking.	• Voices of others are rarely incorporated; the speaker narrates events but seldom, if ever, includes dialogue.	• The emphasis is on learning to work the program, moving past a superficial understanding of the steps, traditions, Big Book, etc.	• The speaker tends to present an idealized view of life in AA.
	• There are frequent confessional interludes.	• The hero is in a process of understanding how he or she has harmed others.	• The speaker eventually begins to construct an idealized portrait of the self in AA, an image that he or she will strive to become.
	• The drunkolog dominates the talk.	• The old-timer who played a role in bringing the speaker to AA is typically idealized.	

harmed others. If they speak about some member of AA who brought them to the program, they will probably idealize that person. They will convey a sense, although not necessarily directly, that they cannot conceive of themselves becoming like that person, becoming like the old-timers in AA.

They will probably say little of the "now," how they have found a new life in AA until later, until they have been in the program longer and until they have begun to change. Even then and for years to come, they will idealize the program and idealize their new lives. When they first speak of their new lives in AA, their voices will probably crack. They may even weep. Their narrative voices, reflecting their current states, may trail behind the idealized images of themselves that they wish to become. They may not yet be convinced that they can change and that their lives can become better.

The Stories of Old-Timers

When old-timers say, "Hello, I'm ———. I'm a grateful alcoholic," newcomers and outsiders might be surprised. How could they be grateful? How could they utter these words with a sense of confidence, acceptance, and maybe even pride? But the audience will come to sense—even if not consciously—that these speakers have assumed a persona. They are not just speaking for themselves. They are speaking for and through the program. And, as they tell their stories, the audience can hear the values of the program, even if they are not yet ready to hear the words and what the words convey. At times, their voices are sermonic, and the audience realizes that there is something spiritual about the speakers and the program. The voices of old-timers are also serene, and the audience realizes that they have moved past a chaotic life destroyed by alcoholism. Throughout, there is laughter, and the audience can begin to experience a community that has found joy where there once was only despair. An old-timer has, in short, a clear voice that carries with it an entire culture, a way of being in the world. This voice is itself a hero or persona or personality, and it will tell of other heroes, speak their words, and reaccentuate them so that those words take on a new meaning.

Old-timers may begin with a brief summary of their childhoods, their lives before they began to drink. Some may not begin here but make brief references to their childhoods throughout their talks. And there is a hero that can only be described as a unique person coming of age in a particular place. Old-timers realize, perhaps not consciously, that this section of the story serves clear rhetorical goals. First, the uniqueness of the hero here will be contrasted to the uniformity of a hero altered by alcoholism, a point developed during the drunkolog. Second, an old-timer describes his or her childhood, family, and environment *without* connect-

The Old-Timer's Story

Narrative Voice

- The voice rises above the events of the talk; its tone is more typically sermonic or serene.
- A persona that represents the values of the program emerges for the speaking voice; it is distinct from the hero of each section.
- Although the speaker might be humorous one moment and serious the next, the voice moves through fewer shifts in emotion.
- Throughout, the speaker demonstrates an understanding of the chronotopes of AA stories.
- The speaker is more likely to quote the Big Book and other program literature from memory.

Childhood	*Drunkolog*	*Coming to AA*	*Now*
• The childhood of the speaker is summarized to convey uniqueness; this uniqueness will be erased as the drunkolog progresses. • The events of childhood are not presented as a cause of drinking.	• The drunkolog occupies less time. • There are few (if any) confessional moments. • The story becomes double voiced as the words of others are incorporated and reaccentuated by the narrative voice. • The hero is the object of parody; events that were once painful to voice are now related with humor. • The speaker makes amends to others by reaccentuating their words and shifting power relations.	• The emphasis is on working the steps. • The speaker is more likely to become didactic, instructing newcomers on the most beneficial ways of working the steps. • The tone in this section might be more sermonic, serious, or reverential than that of the drunkolog.	• The hero, who is portrayed as unfinished, continues to struggle; the speaker may continue to parody the hero. • The emphasis is on helping others, being a sponsor. • The speaker expresses gratitude for the program and a new life.

ing these biographical events to his or her alcoholism. What is perhaps most significant here is what is not said: Old-timers do not connect their childhoods to their drinking.

Old-timers often comment, however, on how they felt different or not normal as a child. Then as they take their first drinks, they feel—for the first time in their lives—normal. The episode of the first drink creates a segue into the drunkolog. For some old-timers, this section of the talk becomes rather short. Even though they still tell their stories in fragments (actually anecdotes that relate specific events), maybe even without placing them in chronological order, there is nonetheless an order. The story is more like autobiography than confession, and the fragments trace the arc of the disease of alcoholism. As old-timers place their heroes (their drinking selves) into this chronotope, they use the inevitable effect of alcoholism to help them move past guilt and shame for their past actions. They even learn to parody the heroes of their drinking days and find humor in events that were once overwhelmingly sad.

What is most striking about the drunkolog of old-timers (and other sections of their talks) is the way voices begin to enter the stories. The talks of newcomers have a single voice. Newcomers might move through a range of emotions, but they do not really create heroes or quote the words of others. We might say that a newcomer has not developed a clear sense of identity within the program and so cannot separate his or her words from the words of others. In the stories of old-timers, we find multiple voices (and clear heroes and dramatis personæ). Bakhtin talks about how the voices in our environment become the voices in our heads, how we need to begin to sort out authoritative voices (voices that demand our belief) and internally persuasive voices (voices that we have critically evaluated and accepted as our own):

> When someone else's ideological discourse is internally persuasive for us and acknowledged by us, entirely different possibilities open up. Such discourse is of decisive significance in the evolution of an individual consciousness: consciousness awakens to independent ideological life precisely in a world of alien discourses surrounding it, and from which it cannot initially separate itself; the process of distinguishing between one's own and another's discourse, between one's own and another's thought, is activated rather late in development. When thought begins to work in an independent, experimenting and discriminating way, what first occurs is a separation between internally persuasive discourse and authoritarian enforced discourse, along with a rejection of those congeries of discourses that do not matter to us, that do not touch us. ("Discourse in the Novel" 345)

In AA, as I wrote earlier, the discourse of meetings, especially the prohibition on cross talk, promotes a separation of voices and allows members to express themselves, without a sideward glance and without a blind acceptance of authoritative discourse. In talks, speakers begin to sort out voices by saying the words of others and reaccentuating them. If speakers say the same words that they said while still drinking in the context of AA, the words take on a new accent and so a new meaning. Speakers frequently parody their former selves by reaccentuating the words that they spoke in the barroom. The speaker might also say the words of a friend or a parent, words they could not believe when they drank, and now reaccentuate them, changing them into words that they can now believe. This, the saying of some other person's words and the reaccentuation of those words, is probably the most remarkable difference between the talks of newcomers and old-timers, and it is more than a simple stylistic feature. It means that the speaker now has developed a clear identity with boundaries.

In the talks of old-timers, the drunkolog does not dominate. The "coming to AA" and "now" sections emerge as more distinct. The "coming to AA" section is likely to be more didactic. Old-timers now have a sophisticated understanding of how to work the program, and they attempt to convey this by talking about how they worked the steps or how they help their sponsees work the steps. In the "now" section, we find an unfinished hero who continues to struggle. The hero that emerges in this section is distinct. The speaking voice, from its position within the program, describes the hero, who continues to struggle, as if he or she were describing someone else. This hero is often the object of parody. Even when this hero is in emotional distress, the speaking voice remains above the turmoil, carrying the message that members of AA can learn to transcend the difficulties of dealing with life on its own terms. Without this message, AA could hardly hope to succeed. Its members came of age by drinking away their pain. Now that they can no longer live in an alcoholic stupor, they must find a new way to deal with the problems and difficulties that all people face. That the program provides an answer is the ultimate message embodied in the voice of old-timers.

A Final Word

I have not, in this book, overtly addressed the critics of AA. Given that the program has been considered the most successful—at least the most visible—means of treating alcoholism for over fifty years, it is not surprising that alternative approaches define themselves, first, by presenting a rather simple and largely unflattering view of AA and, second, by arguing that their program adds a new dimension to the limitations of AA or corrects the weaknesses of AA. They say that AA promotes guilt and shame or that AA is a religious program that cannot serve the "unchurched" drinker. Other critiques come from the outside, perhaps relying on secondhand or thirdhand accounts but typically without making any claim to have studied the culture of AA, perhaps without even citing AA literature. They might say, for example, that AA is an authoritarian organization, that newcomers are forced to work the Twelve Steps, that old-timers demand adherence to the Twelve Traditions, and so on.

This book, a rhetorical analysis of the discourse of AA and its practice of telling stories to change lives, is based on an ethnography of AA. I do not feel that I would have been able to adequately understand my subject without an immersion in the culture of the program. As I came to know the culture of AA more thoroughly, my respect for it grew and criticisms that I encountered struck me as incomplete, trivial, or ill informed. Certainly, newcomers feel guilt and shame, but the program helps them move past it. The program is spiritual, but many members are "unchurched." Old-timers might encourage others to follow the traditions, but they are attempting to provide a bit of stability to a nearly chaotic organization.

I have attempted to present a full analysis—the good and the bad—of what I viewed at AA meetings, but I realize that some might feel that I am overly positive. For those readers who wish to hear more of AA's failings, I would encourage them to enter the carnivalesque world of its meetings and listen. The best critics of AA are its members. Perhaps, this is its greatest strength.

Notes

Works Cited

Index

Notes

Introduction
Bill W.'s Story: An Ethnography of Reading

1. Even from its inception, AA relied upon oral storytelling. Bill W. and Dr. Bob, the cofounders of AA, first met on May 12, 1935, in Akron, Ohio. Newly sober with the help of his friend Edwin T., known as Ebby, and in town on a business trip, Bill felt the need to talk with another alcoholic. Members of the Oxford Group (the connection between the Oxford Group and AA will be discussed in chapter 2) introduced him to Dr. Bob. On June 10, 1935, regarded as the date of AA's origin, Dr. Bob took his last drink. The two soon began to develop their experiences into a program to help other alcoholics. Dr. Bob is generally regarded as playing a stronger role in the actual development of the program, and Bill W. is credited for being the visionary and promoter. (For a history of AA, see Ernest Kurtz's *Not-God*.) The official AA biography of Bill Wilson is *'Pass It On': The Story of Bill Wilson and How the A.A. Message Reached the World*. The official AA biography of Dr. Robert Smith is *Dr. Bob and the Good Oldtimers: A Biography, with Recollections of Early A.A. in the Midwest*.

The oral tradition of AA is what Walter Ong would call "secondary orality," an orality, like electronic media, that has emerged after the advent of literacy. Father Ong writes:

> with telephone, radio, television and various kinds of sound tape, electronic technology has brought us into the age of "secondary orality." This new orality has striking resemblances to the old in its participatory mystique, its fostering of a communal sense, its concentration on the present moment, and even its use of formulas. But it is essentially a more deliberate and self-conscious orality, based permanently on the use of writing and print, which are essential for the manufacture and operation of the equipment and for its use as well. (136)

2. This salutation, which has been adopted almost universally by AA groups in the United States, seems to have developed later in AA history. To be completely accurate, Bill W. may never have uttered the phrase at a meeting. The point I am making here is that current insiders of the program are so used to hearing this salutation at meetings that they read it into the print version.

3. In the early days, the Akron group seems to have been more serious, not encouraging humor or even clapping, but they eventually were influenced by Bill

W.'s more lighthearted approach to sobriety (*Dr. Bob* 221, 223). Among the New York group, under the guidance of Bill W., the use of humor in the telling of one's story was evident even in the early days:

> Those early meetings saw the introduction of some customs so traditional today that their presence—not to mention their origins—is rarely questioned. One of these was the humor—sometimes black, always deeply empathic. This atmosphere of laughter was a direct legacy of Bill's personality. His own talks were always shot through with humor, much of it self-deprecating. Said Ruth: "He could always bring on laughter out of pathos. There would be deep belly laughter." (*'Pass It On'* 219)

4. Throughout this book I will discuss alcoholism as a disease; members of Alcoholics Anonymous believe alcoholism to be a progressive and eventually fatal disease that follows a progressive series of stages that lead to institutionalization in a mental hospital, jail, or death (see Jellinek). While cultural variations (as well as the assumption that "alcoholism" is a social construction that emerged during a specific historical period) should be acknowledged, it should also be pointed out that the "disease" model of AA has been applied cross-culturally. One might argue that the "disease" model must have some material validity for so many members in so many different cultures to find it descriptive of their own experiences. (For a discussion of the cultural/biological controversy, see O'Reilly's *Sobering Tales* 2–5 and Douglas's *Constructive Drinking*.)

5. O'Reilly ties the stock market to the progression of Bill's alcoholism. He writes: "The rise and fall of stocks and money values becomes a leitmotif, replicated in the fluctuations of commercial enterprises, in business successes and failures" (109).

6. In most AA stories, bottoming out is depicted as an egocentric phase. This manifestation of bottoming out might be more typical for extroverts like Bill; Dr. Bob, generally recognized as being more introverted, does not speak of this phase in the same way. Gender differences might also exist. For males, this phase generally takes the form of delusions of grandeur, like Bill's being the "Napoleon of Wall Street." For women, it tends to take the form of withdrawal and self-absorption. Chrouser writes: "Women in recovery are accustomed to seeing themselves as 'inside' a shell" (258). She feels that male AA stories are "grandiose," and female stories are "depressive" (201).

7. In her study of contemporary reading groups, Long comments on how "joining a reading group represents in itself a form of critical reflection on society—or one's place within it—because it demands taking a stance toward a felt lacuna in everyday life and moving toward addressing that gap" (197–98). Characters in books "are often analyzed as if they were real people," which indicated that members analyze the text as a means of creating "equipment for living" rather than as opportunities "of expert display or professional advancement" (199). Similarly, members of AA look to the founders of the program and old-timers as examples of both the difficulties and rewards of sobriety.

8. The friend was Ebby, whom Bill had known since 1911 (*'Pass It On'* 34). Ebby had sobered up through association with the Oxford Group, as will be

discussed in chapter 2. Ebby would later become involved with Alcoholics Anonymous, although he struggled with sobriety and eventually died of the disease (Kurtz 8).

9. Because "circuit speakers" tell their stories at conferences outside of their home districts, maybe speaking as often as once or twice a month, they play an important role in passing on the oral wisdom of the program and in creating a shared culture in an organization that consists of independently functioning groups. To many, they are emblems of success within AA; they are the people who devoted themselves to the program and have, as a result, experienced a great deal of spiritual growth. Many who still struggle with sobriety find the example of these speakers daunting. They feel that circuit speakers idealize life within the program by not adequately treating their current struggles and problems. Certainly, circuit speakers represent a more finely crafted and polished version of storytelling within AA (as will be discussed at a number of points in this book); they typically do not embody many of the more interesting features of storytelling within local meetings, such as confessional moments.

10. It is typical of oral storytelling that certain themes or narrative clusters are stitched together. Even Homer, Father Ong writes, "stitched together prefabricated parts" (22). In AA narratives, the "clusters" that organize the narrative are the drunkolog, coming to AA, and life in AA. As with oral storytelling, the "clusters constitute the organizing principles of the formulas, so that the 'essential idea' is not subject to clear, straightforward formulation but is rather a kind of fictional complex held together largely in the unconscious" (25). In other words, the audience creates a sense of order as they recognize, if only unconsciously, that the speaker is moving in and out of these three basic narrative clusters. Thus, the story need not be told in chronological order for the audience to make chronological sense of it.

1. The Washingtonians: Telling Stories to Teetotalers

1. While alcoholism has arguably always been with us, the recognition of it as a social problem seems to date to the late eighteenth and early nineteenth centuries. Some contributing factors were the development of a medical perspective, beginning with the publication of Benjamin Rush's *An Inquiry into the Effects of Ardent Spirits upon the Human Body* in 1791, the rise of the Industrial Revolution, including the mass production and marketing of spirits and the problems of working with machinery while intoxicated (see O'Reilly, *Sobering Tales* 56), urbanization (see O'Reilly's discussion of Whitman's *Franklin Evans* in his *Sobering Tales* 53–65), and an increasing need to find new means of controlling the working class (see Shields's "The Demonization of the Tavern" and Foucault's *Discipline and Punish*).

2. Until the Washingtonians were formed in 1840, temperance organizations generally believed that drunkards could not be reformed. Maxwell writes, "[T]he temperance movement was aimed solely at keeping the nonalcoholic from becoming an alcoholic" ("Washingtonian" 412).

3. Zug, who was apparently a member of the American Temperance Union and resident of Baltimore, attended early meetings of the Washingtonians and later became a member. He wrote a number of letters about his experience to Rev.

John March, executive secretary of the American Temperance Union (these are quoted in Maxwell, "Washingtonian" 413–14), and later penned *The Foundation, Progress, and Principles of the Washington Temperance Society of Baltimore* (1842), which was apparently written with the approval of the founding members. It is cited here as a statement of the early goals of the movement. The title page of the book is signed "By a Member of the Society." It is copyrighted by John Zug.

4. In the *Twelve Steps and Twelve Traditions*, Bill W. writes of the dangers of becoming involved in both political issues and reform movements:

> In many respects, the Washingtonians were akin to A.A. of today. Their membership passed the hundred thousand mark. Had they been left to themselves, and had they stuck to their one goal, they might have found the rest of the answer. But this didn't happen. Instead, the Washingtonians permitted politicians [including the young Abraham Lincoln] and reformers, both alcoholic and nonalcoholic, to use the society for their own purposes. Abolition of slavery, for example, was a stormy political issue then. Soon, Washingtonian speakers violently and publicly took sides on this question. Maybe the society could have survived the abolition controversy, but it didn't have a chance from the moment it determined to reform America's drinking habits. When the Washingtonians became temperance crusaders, within a very few years they had completely lost their effectiveness in helping alcoholics. (178)

I have not found any evidence that involvement with political issues was a precipitating factor in the demise of the Washingtonians. Bill appears also to have been mistaken about the movement's attitude toward religion. While Zug speaks of the importance of avoiding religion, this seems to have been a goal of the early Baltimore group and not indicative of other groups. Maxwell demonstrates that meetings often included hymns and references to God ("Washingtonian" 437–39); indeed, he cites a "reliance upon the power of God" as one of the common beliefs between the Washingtonians and AA [444]).

5. A member of AA would view Gough's relapses (he had a less sensational relapse shortly after sobering up and then a second that was more compromising and hit the newspapers) as rather unremarkable. While some members sober up and stay sober, most have a few relapses, often with some rather unpleasant consequences. Outsiders to AA tend to view a relapse as a failure; insiders tend to view even one day without drink as a miracle. That Gough had only two relapses (as far as we know) might be considered an exceptional accomplishment. I would also question Reynolds's portrayal of Gough as a disreputable rogue. In my reading of his autobiographies, published lectures, and commentaries on the dangers of alcohol, I felt that he presented—even to a twentieth-century reader—an appealing persona.

6. In the 1845 *Report* to the American Temperance Union, John Marsh wrote that it "has in a considerable measure spent its force" (qtd. in Maxwell, "Washingtonian" 425). The movement's activities may have peaked as early as 1843, and it was virtually defunct by 1858. Even though Hawkins, Gough, and others

referred to themselves as Washingtonians for the rest of their lives, Maxwell finds no mention of the movement or its activities after 1847, except for events in the Boston area ("Washingtonian" 424–26).

7. Most of the tales in volume 1 are told in the first person; the exception is "The Broken Merchant," the longest of the tales in that volume. The tales in volume 2 are told in the third person. It might be argued that the first person tales in volume 1, while certainly altered by Arthur's pen, are a bit closer to the actual tales that he heard at Washingtonian meetings, while those in volume 2 and "The Broken Merchant" are even more extensively influenced by the tradition of temperance literature.

8. While contemporary readers probably considered Grace to be the perfect wife, modern readers might feel she is passive aggressive or controlling, someone who would benefit from attending Al-Anon.

9. Temperance tales were typically about "men at first worthy of envy" whose drinking led to financial ruin and the disruption of their families: "[T]he aim of the temperance movement was to warn that drunkenness caused major social problems by interfering with the natural prosperity which ought to have been the lot of all hardworking males" (Nadelhaft 24). The literature rarely dealt with "the drunken wife" or "the non-violent besotted husband" (25). The bar room was depicted as a "male world" (26).

10. By the time the Washingtonians was formed in 1840, temperance literature had moved from an optimism about "human perfectibility" to a "deepening pessimism" that "reform did not produce lasting results" (Reynolds 66). Arthur's retelling of the Washingtonian stories is an anomaly within this broader trend. When Arthur returned to writing purer temperance tales with *Ten Nights in a Bar-Room,* he returned to the pessimistic view that drink always leads to a deterioration of morals and behavior.

2. The Oxford Group: The Stories of Saints

1. Bill W. wrote to Jung on January 23, 1961, to confirm this story; Jung responded on January 30, 1961. The letters were published, in edited form, in the January 1963 issue of *The A.A. Grapevine* and in *'Pass It On'* (381–85). Interestingly, Rowland's December 22, 1945, obituary in the *New York Times* makes no mention of his contribution to AA.

2. AA's debt to the Oxford Group is a rather complex issue. AA borrowed a number of rituals and beliefs: the importance of a moral inventory and confession, the necessity of giving in to God, allowing one to choose his or her own concept of God, the spiritual need of fellowship, and the belief that one's life can change for the better (Kurtz 17, 48–49). Kurtz cites four negative influences on AA: "Alcoholics Anonymous steadfastly and consistently rejected absolutes, avoided aggressive evangelism, embraced anonymity, and strove to avoid offending anyone who might need its program" (50). Of the founders and their wives, Anne Smith seems to have been the most serious student of the Oxford Group. For her take on the organization, see "Oxford Group Principles" in *Anne Smith's Journal* (127–30).

3. The following works are from Anne Smith's recommended reading list: Begbie's *Life Changers* and *Twice-Born Men;* Shoemaker's *Children of the Sec-*

ond Birth, The Conversion of the Church, and *Twice-Born Ministers;* Reynolds's *New Lives for Old;* Russell's *For Sinners Only;* and Allen's *He That Cometh* (*Anne Smith's Journal* 81–82).

4. The tension between AA and the Oxford Group appears to have been more acute in New York than in Akron. Dr. Bob and the Akron group were slower to break with the Oxford Group and seemed to have retained more of their ideas. For example, in his last talk, Dr. Bob discusses the importance of Absolute Love.

3. Coming to Alcoholics Anonymous: Hearing One's Life in the Voices of Others

1. The source for my description of meetings comes from my own experience attending meetings, listening to speakers (who often discuss what their first meeting was like), and talking to members at "unscheduled" meetings, those meetings that are informal gatherings of people in the program. In order to focus on the most typical events and rituals of AA meetings, I have compared my own experience with the descriptions of meetings in the following dissertations: Nagel's *Identity Reconstruction,* Chrouser's *A Critical Analysis of the Discourse and Reconstructed Stories Shared by Recovering Female Alcoholics in Alcoholics Anonymous,* and Flynn's *Performing Sobriety* (which contains the best and most detailed description of meetings, especially 21–69). I also consulted O'Reilly's *Sobering Tales,* a slight revision of his dissertation.

2. The smoke-filled basement room, occupied by older men, is becoming more and more rare, although it remains the stereotypical image for most outsiders. Today, most meetings occur in banquet rooms of restaurants or rooms rented from churches and are quite pleasant environments.

3. While the hugging is common in most regions, it is not part of the rituals of some meetings.

4. To explain the sponsor/sponsee relationship, I will rely upon *A Sponsorship Guide,* informal conversations with members about their sponsors, and discussions of sponsors that are part of talks. Certainly, the relationship is one of the most private aspects of AA culture; thus, my discussion in this chapter is admittedly limited.

4. Ritualized Reading: The Voices In and Around Sacred Texts

1. Reportedly, the Big Book has sold more copies in Western publishing than any other volume except the Bible and *The Book of Common Prayer.*

2. While there was, initially, some sense that money would be made off the publication of the Big Book (it was independently published by members who bought stock in Works Publishing, Inc., which became A.A. Publishing, Inc. in 1953), it has become an anomaly in the publishing industry. A.A. Publishing sells it at a marginal profit (using the funds to operate AA's central office), and it is distributed at cost by local groups. When I bought my first hardback copy in 1994, it cost $5. At that time, a comparable book sold commercially would have cost in the range of $18 to $25.

3. "J." has offered *A Simple Program,* which is a revision of the Big Book.

5. The Twelve Steps: Finding One's Voice among the Other Voices

1. In contrast to the published version with "we," the manuscript was written with "you" and "must." Before publication, Bill W. distributed four hundred multilith copies for comment. A New Jersey psychiatrist, Dr. Howard, argued that the power of the stories carried such force that the description of the program could be softened by a switch in pronouns (Kurtz 75).

2. Many of the treatment programs offered as alternatives to AA are reactions against the program's emphasis on religion. In *How to Stay Sober: Recovery Without Religion,* James Christopher offers a program for "unchurched" alcoholics. Yet, a large number of AA members are "unchurched," and members often speak of the difference between spirituality and religion.

6. The Twelve Traditions: Bringing a Little Order to Chaos

1. In addition to the Twelve Traditions, groups attain some cohesion through approved publications (the Big Book, *Twelve Steps and Twelve Traditions,* etc., as well as a national newsletter entitled *The Grapevine* and local newsletters), an intergroup and central office (which coordinate district activities), and the General Service Conference, which is attended by a local representative called the general service representative.

2. The traditions are published in long and short versions. I am supplying the short version here; it is the form that is typically read at meetings.

7. The Author and the Hero: Uncertainty, Freedom, and Rigorous Honesty

1. Nothing is pure for Bakhtin. It is characteristic of his thought to set up definitions, assume certain stances, or establish taxonomies that he later moves beyond. Morson and Emerson write that Bakhtin composes essays in the way that polyphonic authors compose novels: "He seems to begin with a set of ideas, which he then passes through several diverse contexts (rather than voices), thus generating new insights to guide his further discussion" (259).

2. While Bakhtin might seem to value the openness of the author over the stasis of the hero, it is important to see both positions as part of a process. Without the stasis of the hero, the author would have no identity. Clark and Holquist write:

> To be open, becoming, is a good thing; it is inseparable from my privilege in existence because it is inseparable from the uniqueness of my self. But as a unique becoming, my I-for-myself is always invisible. In order to perceive that self, it must find expression in categories that can fix it, and these I can only get from the other. So that when I complete the other, or when the other completes me, she and I are actually exchanging the gift of a perceptible self. (79)

Certainly, it is unavoidable that we fix our identity and the identity of others, but it is particularly important that we remind ourselves of the openness of others. Morson writes: "For Bakhtin . . . an ethical approach to other people necessarily involves a recognition of their 'noncoincidence' and 'unfinalizability,' that is, 'their capacity to outgrow, as it were, from within and to render *untrue* any externalizing and finalizing definition of them" ("Prosaic Bakhtin" 65).

3. From Bakhtin's aesthetics emerges his ethics. Patterson writes: "[T]he notion of a 'transgredient self' bears the implication of a transcendent witness, what Bakhtin calls the 'over-I', and this implication introduces a religious dimension to the aesthetic concern—an aspect of Bakhtin's thought frequently overlooked by his interpreters" (55). As we will see, Bakhtin's theory of time and its relation to the author and hero is also inseparable from ethics. Morson writes:

> The openness of time was crucial to Bakhtin because without it there could be neither real ethical choice nor genuine creativity. Ethics and creativity were, in fact, the central concerns of his life. One could view his long career, and his many theories, as different ways of describing the sort of world in which ethics and creativity are not illusory. ("Bakhtin, Genres, and Temporality" 1073)

10. Taking On a New Identity: Faking It to Make It

1. This is similar to Bakhtin's view. While he believes in the importance of the individual and even the expressive element of discourse, Bakhtin is not a Romantic. Clark and Holquist:

> The self/other dichotomy in Bakhtin does not, as in Romantic philosophy, emphasize the self alone, a radical subjectivity always in danger of shading off into solipsistic extremes. For the same reason the self, as conceived by Bakhtin, is not a presence wherein is lodged the ultimate privilege of the real, the source of sovereign intention and guarantor of unified meaning. The Bakhtinian self is never whole, since it can exist only dialogically. (65)

2. In the Oxford Group, the inflated persona (though they do not use this term) was perceived as a major impediment to the development of a spiritual life:

> Every time we try to move forward spiritually that "I" confronts us. It is the fence we put up to mark our very own part of existence from that of other people's when we want to think we are different from everybody else. "I'm sure you can't understand that I am not the same as other people," we say. "I am so very different. I have a good excuse for doing what I did. I know it's no use my explaining to you. But I know what I am." (*What Is the Oxford Group?* 23–24)

3. The notion of alcoholism as a disease is one of the more misunderstood aspects of AA's program. Although the program describes alcoholism as a disease, overtly opposing itself to those who see alcoholism as indicative of a weak will (this notion typically occurs in the drunklog section of talks), the program does not function on a medical model. Except for Silkworth's "The Doctor's Opinion" (*Alcoholics Anonymous* xxiii–xxx), the focus of the Big Book is on the subjective experience of the alcoholic rather than on alcoholism. In AA, alcoholics work a spiritual program; they are not "treated" (see Kurtz 59). (For a discussion

on the disease view of alcoholism by a physician and member of AA, see Dr. Paul O.'s *There's More to Quitting Drinking than Quitting Drinking,* 11–32.)

4. Crapanzano explains:

> The words of one speaker are appropriated by a second speaker as the words of the first speaker but used for the second speaker's own purposes "by inserting a new semantic intention into a discourse which already has, and which retains, an intention of its own." In other words, they are recontextualized, or, in [Linda] Hutcheon's terms, "transcontextualized"—revised, replayed, inverted. Such double-voiced words are—and here I quote [Gary Saul] Morson— "best described not simply as the interaction of two speech acts, but as *an interaction designed to be heard and interpreted by a third person* (or a second 'second person'), whose own process of active reception is anticipated and directed."

Crapanzano points out the this appropriation of the other's words is hierarchical; it "dominates the target" (143); see also Morson and Emerson (154–59). In AA discourse, as I will point out at several points of this analysis, the parody is directed toward the former self (the practicing alcoholic), "alcoholic thinking," or "alcoholic behavior."

11. Confessional Self-Accounting: Speaking *Before* Rather Than *To* an Audience

1. The confessions made during the fifth step might be made once (with particularly sensitive events) or repeatedly (when what is spoken in the fifth step is repeated during topic meetings or speaker meetings). The fifth step is not always taken with one's sponsor; it is sometimes taken with clergy or ministers, especially when the member is confessing past illegal activities.

12. Autobiography: Moving from Isolation and Finding Boundaries

1. Patterson explains the process in this way:

> The author undertakes this project of becoming a self by placing the word into the mouth of the hero like a creator breathing a soul into his creature. And the breath he breathes is the breath he draws; dialogically generating a presence in relation to his hero, the author is summoned as he summons. This splitting of the self is a wounding of the self, and from that wound which tears the self away from itself the hero emerges, as from a womb. (59)

2. Chrouser has argued the opposite, that "acceptance of the new identity is contingent upon rejection of the old identity" (73). Her view is more typical of the theory of personal narrative and autobiography, which emphasizes radical splits between the "before self" and the "after self."

3. The concentration of a speaker on the drunkolog might seem problematic: Why do recovering alcoholics talk so much of their drinking days? This is often explained as meeting the needs of aesthetic narration. As O'Reilly says, "stories

about drinking seem to be more interesting than stories about not drinking" (*Sobering Tales* 98). I would argue that the portion of the narrative devoted to the drunkolog serves a rhetorical purpose for the audience (it is a hook for newcomers, creating a sense of shared identity) and speaker (who needs, as I discuss above, to keep the old self alive in order to create a distance from the former self and stabilize the new identity). Certainly, the drunkolog tends to be longer for newcomers; the newcomer might also reflect more of a drinking self boastfulness about drinking exploits and even a mournful regret about the past life. Old-timers tend to spend less time on the drunkolog and, as I have said elsewhere in this book, employ more irony and humor.

4. Morson and Emerson write: "For Dostoevsky as Bakhtin understands him, and for Bakhtin himself, 'secondhand' definitions of others are fundamentally unethical. One must approach another as a 'personality,' that is, as someone 'who has not yet uttered his ultimate word'" (265). This is, essentially, what the polyphonic author of the novel does. The polyphonic author is not seduced by the surplus ("I know this other as he or she cannot know himself or herself") but recognizes his "outsideness" and the limits of the "surplus." Thus, the author accepts "the other's capacity for change" (242). A number of factors in AA stories support what Bakhtin would consider to be the ethical narration of others: the establishment of boundaries between self and others, the focus on the development of self, the discouragement of judging or blaming others, and the attempt to come to a provisional and limited understanding of others. Indeed, others play a remarkably minor role in AA stories.

5. Patterson writes of Bakhtin's "Author and Hero," using, as did Burke, the metaphor of death: "In order to live as I, the author must become *other* to himself. For what has been said, one sees that the highest expression of this movement of the I is a being for death which is a dying away from the self for the sake of other" (60).

13. Chronotopes: The Order Behind Fragments of a Life

1. In "Author and Hero in Aesthetic Activity," Bakhtin argues that autobiography emerges in the early Renaissance from confessional self-accounting (150). In "Forms of Time and Chronotope in the Novel," a later work, Bakhtin discusses much earlier forms of autobiography (130–46).

2. Frank Kermode believes that any full narrative necessarily entails secrets: "Secrets . . . are at odds with sequence, which is considered as an aspect of propriety; and a passion for sequence may result in the suppression of the secret" (83–84). In autobiography, as I explained in the last chapter, these secrets can destabilize the hero and the text. In AA storytelling, secrets serve to establish boundaries. Bill W., for example, only briefly mentions his wife as he tells his story in chapter one of the Big Book. One might ask, what is he hiding? Within the discourse of AA, the answer is simple: It's none of your business.

3. To explain the concept of a "surplus of seeing," Morson uses the example of foreshadowing. Because the author knows the fate of the hero, he or she can foreshadow the end. In contrast, Morson cites Tolstoy's process of composing *War and Peace* in serialization. Tolstoy wrote each installment "without knowing what was going to happen to his characters" in the next installment; he

planned to end the novel by simply stopping after one of the installments. Morson argues that the hero, when ethically constructed, will surprise the author and the reader ("Bakhtin, Genres, and Temporality").

4. In *John Barleycorn,* Jack London calls such moments "White Logic." O'Reilly explains:

> The White Logic teaches that intrinsic value is absent in the cosmos and that human value systems are cobbled together out of social fictions, aesthetic illusions, and the falsifications of need. Man, the White Logic tells London, is a "flux of states of consciousness, a flow of passing thoughts, each thought of self another self, a myriad thoughts, a myriad selves, a continual becoming but never being, a will-o'-the-wisp flitting of ghosts in ghostland." (*Sobering Tales* 72)

O'Reilly calls this cynicism a "rhetorical immunization procedure intended to strengthen both writer and reader as it dilutes the toxin of terror and solitude" (73). To paraphrase, in moments of clarity, when alcoholics see their lives as they really are, they "immunize" themselves against despair of their lives by saying all life has no meaning.

5. O'Reilly makes this point when discussing London's *John Barleycorn:*

> London does not render John Barleycorn in full allegorical array, yet "he" is kept a sufficient distance from the realm of abstraction and critical analysis to enable the writer to resist comprehending "him" as internal or systemic. Of course London means to dramatize the awesome power of alcohol—but here is precisely the issue: the dramatization has already happened, not as an artistic act but as an epistemological error supported by the popular culture. Intoxication has already been identified as a quantifiable substance outside the self, an external thing that resides in bottles and barrels, with its own life force and the will to compel submission. (*Sobering Tales* 66–67)

6. In "Twisted Tales," Nelson Goodman analyzes the "narratives" of paintings to argue that narrative elements can be jumbled considerably without destroying the narrative: "These varied verbal and pictorial examples show that in a narrative neither the telling nor what is explicitly told need take time, and they suggest furthermore that narrative reordering in any way at all is still narrative" (110–11). In this sense, one could argue that AA stories are typically "twisted" narratives with a plot that is largely constructed by the auditors. Nonetheless, Goodman agrees with my point here, that a clean narrative is normative and that "twisted" tales are more likely to be transformative. He writes: "World structure is heavily dependent on order of elements and on comparative weight of kinds; and reordering and weight shifting are among the most powerful processes used in making and remaking facts and worlds" (115).

7. White writes:

> If every fully realized story, however we define that familiar but conceptually elusive entity, is a kind of allegory, points to a moral, or endows events, whether real or imaginary, with a significance that

they do not possess as a mere sequence, then it seems possible to conclude that every historical narrative has as its latent or manifest purpose the desire to *moralize* the events of which it treats. (13–14)

8. O'Reilly writes: "The process of hearing what one needs to hear by listening to one's own story as it is spoken has its reciprocal in the experience of hearing one's own story told by another speaker" (*Sobering Tales* 143). Flynn writes:

Most of the AA stories I have reviewed reflect that participation by being filled with those "absent others." The stories of many other alcoholics, through a special kind of "ghostwriting", are twined around each speaker's own recovery story to produce a thread which is, in turn, woven into the immense tapestry that is the larger story of AA. (92)

It is important, also, to note that speakers often make comments about how their own life stories do not fit the typical AA story.

Works Cited

Alcoholics Anonymous Comes of Age: A Brief History. New York: Alcoholics Anonymous, 1957.

Alcoholics Anonymous: The Story of How Many Thousands of Men and Women Have Recovered from Alcoholism. 1939. 3rd ed. New York: Alcoholics Anonymous World Services, 1976.

Arthur, T. S. *Temperance Tales; or, Six Nights with the Washingtonians.* 2 vols. Philadelphia: T. B. Peterson, 1871.

———. *Ten Nights in a Bar-Room.* 1854. *"Ten Nights in a Bar-Room" and "In His Steps."* Ed. C. Hugh Holman. New York: Odyssey, 1966.

B., Lisa. AA Talk. August 2, 1996. Springfield, MO: Jody's Tapes, n.d.

Bakhtin, M. M. *Art and Answerability: Early Philosophical Essays by M. M. Bakhtin.* Trans. Vadim Liapunov. Ed. Michael Holquist and Vadim Liapunov. Austin: U of Texas P, 1990.

———. "Author and Hero in Aesthetic Activity." *Art and Answerability* 4–256.

———. "The *Bildungsroman* and Its Significance in the History of Realism (Toward a Historical Typology of the Novel)." *Speech Genres* 10–59.

———. *The Dialogic Imagination: Four Essays.* Trans. Caryl Emerson and Michael Holquist. Ed. Michael Holquist. Austin: U of Texas P, 1981.

———. "Discourse in the Novel." *The Dialogic Imagination* 259–422.

———. "Forms of Time and Chronotope in the Novel." *The Dialogic Imagination* 84–258.

———. "From the Prehistory of Novelistic Discourse." *The Dialogic Imagination* 41–83.

———. "The Problem of Speech Genres." *Speech Genres* 60–102.

———. "The Problem of the Text." *Speech Genres* 103–31.

———. *Problems of Dostoevsky's Poetics.* Trans. and ed. Caryl Emerson. Minneapolis: U of Minnesota P, 1984.

———. *Rabelais and His World.* Trans. Hélène Iswolsky. Bloomington: Indiana UP, 1984.

———. "Response to a Question from the *Novy Mir* Editorial Staff." *Speech Genres* 1–7.

———. *Speech Genres and Other Late Essays.* Trans. Vern W. McGee. Ed. Caryl Emerson and Michael Holquist. Austin: U of Texas P, 1986.

———. "Toward a Methodology for the Human Sciences." *Speech Genres* 159–72.

———. *Toward a Philosophy of the Act.* Trans. Vadim Liapunov. Ed. Vadim Liapunov and Michael Holquist. Austin: U of Texas P, 1993.

Bateson, Gregory. "The Cybernetics of 'Self': A Theory of Alcoholism." *Steps to an Ecology of Mind: Collected Essays in Anthropology, Psychiatry, Evolution, and Epistemology.* San Francisco: Chandler, 1972. 309–37.

Bernard-Donals, Michael. "Mikhail Bakhtin, Classical Rhetoric, and Praxis." *Rhetoric Society Quarterly* 22 (1992): 10–15.

Bob, Dr. AA Talk. 1949. Moore, OK: Soolner Cassette, n.d.

Boyarin, Jonathan, ed. *The Ethnography of Reading.* Berkeley: U of California P, 1992.

———. "Jewish Ethnography and the Question of the Book." *Anthropological Quarterly* 64 (1991): 14–29.

———. "Voices Around the Text: The Ethnography of Reading at Mesivta Tifereth Jerusalem." Boyarin, *Ethnography of Reading* 212–37.

Burke, Kenneth. *A Rhetoric of Motives.* 1950. Berkeley: U of California P, 1962.

Christopher, James. *How to Stay Sober: Recovery Without Religion.* Amherst, MA: Prometheus, 1988.

Chrouser, Kelley Renee. "A Critical Analysis of the Discourse and Reconstructed Stories Shared by Recovering Female Alcoholics in Alcoholics Anonymous." Diss. U of Nebraska, 1990.

Clark, Katerina, and Michael Holquist. *Mikhail Bakhtin.* Cambridge: Harvard UP, 1984.

Crapanzano, Vincent. "The Postmodern Crisis: Discourse, Parody, Memory." Mandelker 137–50.

D., Ken. AA Talk. June 1995. Moore, OK: Sooner Cassette, n.d.

Dannenbaum, Jed. *Drink and Disorder: Temperance Reform in Cincinnati from the Washingtonian Revival to the WCTU.* Urbana: U of Illinois P, 1984.

Dostoevsky, Fyodor. "Notes from the Underground." *Great Short Works of Fyodor Dostoevsky.* New York: Perennial, 1968. 261–378.

Douglas, Mary, ed. *Constructive Drinking: Perspectives on Drink from Anthropology.* Cambridge, MA: Cambridge UP, 1987.

Dr. Bob and the Good Oldtimers: A Biography with Recollections of Early A.A. in the Midwest. New York: Alcoholics Anonymous World Services, 1980.

Emerson, Caryl. *The First Hundred Years of Mikhail Bakhtin.* Princeton: Princeton UP, 1997.

Exley, Frederick. *A Fan's Notes: A Fictional Memoir.* New York: Vintage, 1968.

Fabian, Johannes. "Keep Listening: Ethnography and Reading." Boyarin, *Ethnography of Reading* 80–97.

———. "Text as Terror: Second Thoughts about Charisma." *Social Research* 46 (1979): 166–203.

Fitzgerald, Robert. *The Soul of Sponsorship: The Friendship of Fr. Ed Dowling, S.J. and Bill Wilson in Letters.* Center City, MN: Hazelden, 1995.

Flynn, Kathleen Anne. "Performing Sobriety: Story and Celebration in Alcoholics Anonymous." Diss. Northwestern U, 1994.

Foucault, Michel. *Discipline and Punish: The Birth of the Prison.* 1975. Trans. Alan Sheridan. New York: Random, 1977.

Fox, Emmet. *The Sermon on the Mount.* New York: Grosset and Dunlap, 1938.

Goodman, Nelson. "Twisted Tales; or, Story, Study, and Symphony." *On Narrative.* Mitchell 99–115.

H., Ted. AA Talk. August 5, 1995. Springfield, MO: Ozarks Recordings & More!, n.d.

Hamill, Pete. *A Drinking Life: A Memoir.* Boston: Little, Brown, 1994.

Holman, C. Hugh. Preface. *Ten Nights in a Bar-Room.* By T. S. Arthur.

Holquist, Michael. "Bakhtin and Rabelais: Theory as Praxis." *Boundary* 11 (1982–83): 5–19.

"J." *A Simple Program: A Contemporary Translation of the Book "Alcoholics Anonymous."* New York: Hyperion, 1966.

James, William. *The Varieties of Religious Experience: A Study in Human Nature.* New York: Longmans, Green, 1902.

Jellinek, Elvin Morton. "Phases of Alcohol Addition." *Society, Culture, and Drinking Patterns.* Ed. David J. Pittman and Charles R. Snyder. Carbondale: Southern Illinois UP, 1962. 356–68.

Jung, C. G. *The Collected Works of C.G. Jung.* 20 vols. Ed. Herbert Read, Michael Fordham, Gerhard Adler, and William McGuire. Princeton: Princeton UP, 1959, 1969.

———. *Modern Man in Search of a Soul.* Trans. W. S. Dell and Cary F. Baynes. New York: Harvest, 1933.

K., Gail. AA Talk. August 5, 1995. Springfield, MO: Ozarks Recordings & More!, n.d.

K., Michael. "The Rhetoric of *I Am an Alcoholic:* Three Perspectives." *Rhetorical Society Quarterly* 17 (1987): 151–66.

Kermode, Frank. "Secrets and Narrative Sequence." Mitchell 79–97.

Klancher, Jon. "Bakhtin's Rhetoric." *Reclaiming Pedagogy: The Rhetoric of the Classroom.* Ed. Patricia Donahue and Ellen Quandahl. Carbondale: Southern Illinois UP, 1989. 83–96.

Klein, Anne Carolyn. "Oral Genres and the Art of Reading in Tibet." *Oral Tradition* 9 (1994): 281–314.

Knapp, Carolyn. *Drinking: A Love Story.* New York: Delta, 1997.

Kurtz, Ernest. *Not-God: A History of Alcoholics Anonymous.* Center City, MN: Hazelden, 1979.

Long, Elizabeth. "Textual Interpretation as Collective Action." Boyarin, *Ethnography of Reading* 180–301.

M., Dick. AA Talk. March 19, 1991. Rogersville, MO: Ted Inc. Cassettes, n.d.

Mandelker, Amy, ed. *Bakhtin in Contexts: Across the Disciplines.* Introduction by Caryl Emerson. Evanston, IL: Northwestern UP, 1995.

Maxwell, Milton A. "Alcoholics Anonymous." *Alcohol Science and Society Revisited.* Ed. Edith Lisansky Gomber, Helene Raskin White, and John A. Carpenter. Ann Arbor: U of Michigan P, 1982.

———. "The Washingtonian Movement." *Quarterly Journal of Studies on Alcohol* 11 (1950): 410–51.

McClellan, William. "The Dialogic Other: Bakhtin's Theory of Rhetoric." *Discourse Social/Social Discourse* 3 (1990): 233–49.

Mitchell, W. J. T., ed. *On Narrative.* Chicago: U of Chicago P, 1980.

Morson, Gary Saul. "Bakhtin, Genres, and Temporality." *New Literary History* 22 (1991): 1071–92.

———. "Prosaic Bakhtin: *Landmarks,* Anti-Intelligentsialism, and the Russian Countertradition." Mandelker 33–78.

Morson, Gary Saul, and Caryl Emerson. *Mikhail Bakhtin: Creation of a Prosaics.* Stanford: Stanford UP, 1990.

N., Carolyn. AA Talk. December 6, 1996. Springfield, MO: Jody's Tapes, n.d.

Nadelhaft, Jerome. "Alcohol and Wife Abuse in Antebellum Male Temperance Literature." *Canadian Review of American Studies* 25 (1995): 15–43.

Nagel, George, Jr. "Identity Reconstruction: Communication and Storytelling in Alcoholics Anonymous." Diss. U of Utah, 1988.

O., Paul, Dr. AA Talk. June 1995. Moore, OK: Sooner Cassette, n.d.

——. *There's More to Quitting Drinking than Quitting Drinking.* Laguna Niguel, CA: Sabrina, 1995.

O'K., Ray. AA Talk. August 2, 1992. Rogersville, MO: Ted Inc. Cassettes, n.d.

Ong, Walter J. *Orality and Literacy: The Technologizing of the Word.* London: Methuen, 1982.

O'Reilly, Edmund Bernard. *Sobering Tales: Narratives of Alcoholism and Recovery.* Amherst: U of Massachusetts P, 1997.

——. "Toward Rhetorical Immunity: Narratives of Alcoholism and Recovery." Diss. U of Pennsylvania, 1988.

Palmer, R. Barton. "Languages and Power in the Novel: Mapping the Monologic." *Studies in the Literary Imagination* 23 (1990): 99–127.

'Pass It On': The Story of Bill Wilson and How the A.A. Message Reached the World. New York: Alcoholics Anonymous World Services, 1984.

Patterson, David. "The Religious Aspect of Bakhtin's Aesthetics." *Renascence* 46 (1993): 55–70.

Reynolds, David S. *Beneath the American Renaissance: The Subversive Imagination in the Age of Emerson and Melville.* New York: Knopf, 1988.

Reynolds, David S., and Debra J. Rosenthal. *The Serpent in the Cup: Temperance in American Literature.* Amherst: U of Massachusetts P, 1997.

Roth, Lillian. *Beyond My Worth.* New York: Frederick Fell, 1958.

——. *I'll Cry Tomorrow.* With Mike Connolly and Gerold Frank. New York: Frederick Fell, 1954.

Rush, Benjamin. *An Inquiry into the Effects of Spirituous Liquors on the Human Body, to Which Is Added a Moral and Physical Thermometer.* Boston: Thomas & Andrews, 1791.

Russell, A. J. *For Sinners Only: The Book of the Oxford Groups.* New York: Harper, 1932.

Sánchez-Eppler, Karen. "Temperance in the Bed of a Child: Incest and Social Order in Nineteenth-Century America." Reynolds and Rosenthal 60–92.

Schuster, Charles I. "Mikhail Bakhtin: Philosopher of Language." *The Philosophy of Discourse: The Rhetorical Turn in Twentieth-Century Thought.* Vol. 2. Ed. Chip Sills and George H. Jensen. Portsmouth, NH: Boynton/Cook, Heinemann, 1992. 164–98.

Shields, David S. "The Demonization of the Tavern." Reynolds and Rosenthal 10–21.

Smith, Anne. *Anne Smith's Journal: A.A.'s Principles of Success.* Ed. Dick B. San Rafael, CA: Paradise, 1992.

Svenbro, Jesper. "The 'Voice' of Letters in Ancient Greece: On Silent Reading and the Representation of Speech." *Culture and History* 2 (1987): 31–47.

T., M. *A Sponsorship Guide for All Twelve-Step Programs: Advice for Recovery Related Problems.* Palm Beach, FL: PT Publications, 1995.

Todorov, Tzvetan. *Genres in Discourse.* 1978. Cambridge: Cambridge UP, 1990.

Twelve Steps and Twelve Traditions. New York: Alcoholics Anonymous World Services, 1952.

Twenty-Four Hours a Day. New York: Dodd, Mead, 1975.

W., Bill. AA Talk. 1960. Moore, OK: Sooner Cassette, n.d.

———. Letter to Al. May 22, 1942. Alcoholics Anonymous Archives. General Service Office of Alcoholics Anonymous, New York.

———. Letter to John F. May 14, 1957. Alcoholics Anonymous Archives.

———. Letter to Charles H. November 17, 1953. Alcoholics Anonymous Archives.

———. Letter to Larry J. June 27, 1940. Alcoholics Anonymous Archives.

———. Letter to Larry J. June 9, 1942. Alcoholics Anonymous Archives.

———. Letter to Lois K. January 3, 1951. Alcoholics Anonymous Archives.

———. Letter to Frank L. June 24, 1949. Alcoholics Anonymous Archives.

———. Letter to Milton A. Maxwell. August 12, 1950. Alcoholics Anonymous Archives.

———. Letter to Don R. July 21, 1965. Alcoholics Anonymous Archives.

———. Letter to Clarian S. December 15, 1950. Alcoholics Anonymous Archives.

———. Letter to Sam Shoemaker. June 27, 1949. Alcoholics Anonymous Archives.

———. Letter to Sam Shoemaker. July 14, 1949. Alcoholics Anonymous Archives.

———. Letter to Sam Shoemaker. July 27, 1953. Alcoholics Anonymous Archives.

———. Letter to Sam Shoemaker. February 7, 1957. Alcoholics Anonymous Archives.

———. Letter to Sam Shoemaker. April 23, 1963. Alcoholics Anonymous Archives.

———. Letter to Spence. June 18, 1962. Alcoholics Anonymous Archives.

———. Letter to Ted. March 25, 1940. Alcoholics Anonymous Archives.

What Is the Oxford Group? London: Oxford UP/Humphrey Milford, 1933.

White, Eugene. *Puritan Rhetoric: The Issue of Emotion in Religion.* Carbondale: Southern Illinois UP, 1972.

White, Hayden. "The Value of Narrativity in the Representation of Reality." Mitchell 1–23.

[Zug, John.] *The Foundation, Progress, and Principles of the Washington Temperance Society of Baltimore, and the Influence It Has Had on the Temperance Movements in the United States.* Baltimore: John D. Toy, 1842.

Index

George H. Jensen is a professor of English at Southwest Missouri State University. His books include *Arthur Miller: A Bibliographical Checklist; Personality and the Teaching of Composition* (with John K. DiTiberio); *From Texts to Text: Mastering Academic Writing; The Philosophy of Discourse: The Rhetorical Turn in Twentieth-Century Thought* (edited with Chip Sills); and *Personality and Writing: Finding Your Style, Your Voice, Your Way* (with John K. DiTiberio).